THE TIBETAN WORLD OF THE INDIAN HIMALAYAS

The Tibetan World of the Indian Himalayas

An Ethnography of the 'Garden of Dakini'

TANASE JIRO

MANOHAR
2012

First published 2012

ISBN 978-81-7304-957-6

Published by
Ajay Kumar Jain *for*
Manohar Publishers & Distributors
4753/23 Ansari Road, Daryaganj
New Delhi 110 002

Typeset by
Umesh Chand Nailwal
Delhi 110 092

Printed at
Salasar Imaging Systems
Delhi 110 035

Contents

CHAPTER 1

Introduction: The Land of Lahul or Garsha Khandoling: Where the Tibetan and Hindu Worlds Meet

The region within Central Asia where the Tibetan people live and where the Buddhist Tibetan culture has primarily permeated, is truly vast.

On the Tibetan Plateau, north of the Himalayan range, lies the central basin of the Yarlung Tsangpo River. The eastern region of this basin, centred around the Dalai Lama's capital of Lhasa (lha sa), is called U(dbus), while the western area, around Shigatse (gzi ka rtse)—where the Tashilhunpo (bkra shis lhung po) monastery is located, is called Tsang (gtsang). Although both of these regions now form part of the Tibet Autonomous Region of China, U-Tsang can be considered the centre of the Tibetan cultural sphere.

Even now, vast areas of Asia are strongly influenced by Tibetan culture. These include Mongolia to the north, the Himalayan state of Bhutan and the Indian state of Sikkim to the south, western Sichuan to the east, and in the west, the Indian states of Jammu & Kashmir and a part of Himachal Pradesh (see Map 1). Tibetan cultural influence has also spread to the republics of Buryatia, Tuva and Kalmykia of Russia.

Lahul, the land I will be introducing in this book, lies near the south-western edge of this vast Tibetan cultural domain, and is now a part of the Indian state of Himachal Pradesh (see Map 2). It is situated in the region centred

Map 1: India and Himachal Pradesh

Map 2: Himachal Pradesh

around the 77 °E longitude and the 32.5 °N latitude, and belongs to the area called Punjab-Himalaya within the Himalayan mountain range. It covers 5,830 sq km, but has a population of only around 20,000 people.

The people of Lahul live on a highland which is 3,400 m above sea level in a cold and harsh mountainous environment. Much of the year it is cut-off from the outside world. The pass that provides access to the area is usually closed from November through June, with travel outside of Lahul during those months only possible by helicopter or on foot through dangerous snowfields.

Villages line the steep gorges created by the Chandra and Bhaga rivers, and the Chandra-Bhaga River formed by the confluence of the two. Which flow through the Lahul region (the Chandra-Bhaga River becomes the Chenab downstream in Pakistan, then eventually joins the Indus before flowing into the Arabian Sea). Tibetans know this area as Garsha Kandolin (gar zha mka' 'gro ling).

COMPLEX SOCIAL CONDITIONS

Although it is a small geographical area, very complex social conditions are found in Lahul. According to the well-known Indian linguist D.D. Sharma, there are seven groups with different languages living in the Lahul area:[1] For instance, in the Bhaga basin (the main focus of this book), the area called Punam, which stretches from the Tandi downstream to the Peukar upstream (see Map 3), has its own language. It has been associated with Munda, the language of the indigenous people of India,[2] and belongs to a completely different language genealogy from the Tibetan dialect used in Tod (Stod) region, which lies upstream from Punam. The differences between the two languages are quite striking. For example, the villages of

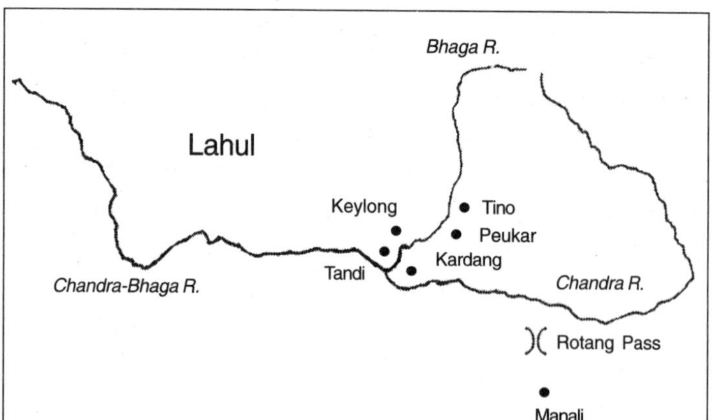

Map 3: Villages of Lahul

Peukar in Punam and Tino in Tod are only a few kilometres apart, both being located on the left bank of the Bhaga River, and there are no distinctions in their cultural characteristics such as clothing, customs of daily life or housing styles. However, the languages spoken in these villages are completely different from one another.

To all outward appearances these people seem to belong to the same society and culture. So, this raises the question, how did such a remarkable linguistic break occur between two villages located so close to each other? For a Japanese like me who grew up in a homogeneous linguistic environment, this situation is hard to understand, but the people in Punam define themselves as Punampa specifically because of the language they speak. At the same time, however, they have kept their cultural identity as Lahulian or Garshan (gar zha pa) along with the people of Tod and others around them. Women wearing fitted trousers under long pleated skirts in sober colours such as dark brown or navy blue and a vest are a unique sight in this particular region. Although they acknowledge the deep connections with Tibet in their religion and other cultural features, they consider themselves different from the people of Bopa (Tibetan) or Khampa (eastern Tibetan, although in Lahul this word often refers to the Tibetan people in general).

HISTORY OF LAHUL

One reason for such complex cultural conditions in Lahul is that this land is clearly a cultural and political intersection between the Tibetan and Hindu spheres. Indeed, between the twelfth and seventeenth centuries, Lahul came under the control of the kingdom of Ladakh in the north, and then under the jurisdiction of the Hindu kingdom of Kullu or Chamba. In more recent times it was integrated into

British India–the Republic of India–except for a short period of domination by the Sikhs.[3]

During the British Indian period, the colonial government retained and utilized the existing ruling structure of Lahul. Feudal lords called Jo, or Thakurs, were appointed as local governors by the Indian government, and handled various duties related to administration, justice and tax collection.

During this period, in 1856, the Moravian Mission established its base at Keylong in Lahul. In 1857, Heinrich August Jaschke (1817-83) was assigned to this post as a missionary. He studied the Tibetan language and later completed a Tibetan dictionary, which is still in use today, as well as a Tibetan translation of the Bible. In 1906, August Hermann Francke (1870-1930), who contributed greatly to the research of Western Tibetan history, was also posted at Keylong. In brief, during this specific period, Lahul was the frontier of Tibetan studies for the West.[4] However, there were hardly any conversions to Christianity in Lahul.

After the Second World War, following Independence in 1947, the power of the long-established chiefs was forfeited. Since Tibet was occupied by China in 1959, Lahul was forced to be integrated into the Indian society, and the influence of India has been growing steadily.

Considering the background of this region, there are good reasons for referring to Lahul as the 'Tibetan World of Indian Himalaya'. Geographically, Lahul lies next to the areas such as Zanskar and Spiti, the people follow a Tibetan lifestyle that is suited to the high altitude, and, as I will note later, incorporates customs and concepts unique to Tibetan culture, such as polyandry and the concept of 'bone and flesh'. It is also permeated by Tibetan Buddhism.

Perhaps it is also appropriate to consider Lahul a part of the southern edge of the Tibetan cultural sphere, along with Bhutan, Sikkim, Mustang, Ladakh, Zanskar and Spiti. Since these areas have been strongly influenced by Tibetan culture, yet imbued with the cultural elements unique to the land, such as Hinduism, they have developed societies with their own characteristics.

However, people who actually live in a society unconcerned about the issue of determining to which civilization their society really belongs to. People integrate the traditional values they inherit from their ancestors with new emerging value systems, facing the situations that confront them, and get on with their lives.

In this book, I want to illustrate how the people of Lahul have invented various ingenious measures to cope with the harsh environment, managed to develop rich human relations, and deal with the tensions caused by such conditions, as well as religious passions which occasionally arise among these steadfast villagers.

I will briefly outline the structure of this book according to its division into the following chapters. Chapter 2 provides a simple description of Kardang village where I spent most of my time in the Lahul region. In Chapter 3 I will focus on the economy, specifically on the main traditional livelihoods of agriculture and stock farming. Chapters 4 through 6 discuss the social structure of Lahul. The central theme is the issue of opposing principles between the household (*kyum*) and the family (*jinmad*). I will discuss various topics such as the means of inheriting wealth, issues of marriage and adopting a bridegroom (*makpa*) into the bride's family, and gender issues.

In Chapter 7, I will introduce indigenous supernatural beings such as earth spirits and evil spirits. Because these spirits can create havoc with village life by occasionally causing villagers to commit murders, these entities can sometimes assume a more powerful reality than the divine deities of Buddhism.

In Chapter 8 I will take up the subject of a religious utopian movement that developed in the Lahul region during the early 1960s. The leader of this movement was Terton Tulshuk Lingpa, a Ningmapa *yogi* from Tibet. Lahul has existed within the vast Tibetan cultural area, and ascetics such as Tulshuk Lingpa, as well as various pilgrims and traders, have travelled throughout the land.

A religious movement called Rime that previously sprang up in Tibet touched off the resurgence of Buddhism in Lahul during the previous century.

In Chapter 9, I will summarize the religious activities in Lahul with reference to the Tibetan context, whilst also noting the most recent changes.

NOTES

1. Sharma, 1989.
2. Francke, 1977 (1907), pp. 171-9, or Grieson, 1967 (1908), vol. 3, part 1, pp. 69-71, 427-9, 453-77.
3. Hutchson and Vogel 1982 (1933), vol. 2, pp. 474-83.
4. Bray, 1998.

CHAPTER 2

Kardang Village

INITIAL FIELD RESEARCH

The gateway to Lahul is Manali, now the largest resort city in northern India. Lying in the deepest reaches of the Kullu valley, the town was once most known for its timber and apples. Recently, it has become a summer resort for people escaping the heat of the Indian plains, especially just before the monsoon season.

The road from Manali to Lahul passes through a coniferous forest, before beginning its steep and meandering ascent toward the Rothang Pass. At a height of about 4,000 m, this pass represents the cultural boundary separating the Tibetan cultural areas of Ladakh, Zanskar, Spiti and Lahul from the Hindu cultural world in India.

As one cross over the Rothang Pass, impressive mountain ranges scoured by glaciers come into view. The road then descends into the deep gorge created by the Chandra River. Tibetan people call this land Garsha Kandoling, means 'Garden of Dakini'. In Tibetan religious tales, *dakinis* are depicted as beautiful goddesses who take on the important role of guiding practitioners or delivering sacred messages. The real reason why this place is called by such a romantic name is a mystery to me.

Furthermore, Lahul is known as a place of pilgrimage among Tibetans due to Garsha Pagpa (gar zha 'phags pa), the holy place for Avalokitesvara (sphyan ras gzigs), and the sacred Dilburi (dril bu ri) mountain.[1]

I first arrived in this land in mid-July of 1987. Previously, a Tibetan acquaintance had introduced me to a village called Kardang that sits across from Lahul's central town of Keylong. I can still remember the first time I set eyes on the village of Kardang. Under a cloudy sky, the greyish-brown clay walled buildings were huddled close together on the middle of a steep slope on the left bank of the Bhaga River. From a distance they created an image of an old abandoned fort. The feeling of being surrounded by a kind of eerie force mingled with the tension I felt about working in the field for the first time.

PEOPLE OF KARDANG VILLAGE

Fortunately, I had the opportunity to live with the Karpa family in Kardang village. At that time the household comprised nine members: the parents, their four sons, the wife of the eldest son, and two grandchildren.

Dorje, the head of the Karpa household (called the *yonda*), was nearly 60 years old. He was a likable person with a thin moustache.

Dorje's wife Palmo was responsible for managing the home as the housewife (known as the *yondamo*). As I will elaborate later, given that the housewife has considerable authority over family matters, the old-fashioned Japanese word *ie-toji* (matriarch) is a much more fitting description for her role than 'housewife'. Our matriarch Palmo was also a quite a responsible character.

Dorje and Palmo's eldest son Ulgyan was of a rather slight build and worked as a tailor in the nearby town of Keylong. His wife, Norpalzom came from the neighbouring village of Guazang. In Lahul many couples get married after dating for a while, but in this case the marriage was arranged with the mutual consent of both families. As is the rule for the women of Lahul, she was a hard worker, and possessed striking dark eyes.

Ulgyan's younger brother, the second son Tashi, was the most handsome amongst the brothers, and we later became close friends. Handsome men often tend to be vain but, refreshingly, he did not have this trait.

The third son, Sonam, was a monk and usually stayed in the monastery above the village. Later he went into a three-year and three-month indoor meditation practice, which is part of the training in the Kagyu school of Tibetan Buddhism, so I was no longer able to see him. For reasons unknown to me, he was the only brother who seemed rather glum.

The youngest son, Pannaral, was a tall, thin young man. At that time he was studying at a college in the Punjab capital, Chandigarh, and came home only during the holidays. Following his graduation he became a highly paid bank employee.

Dorje and Palmo also had a daughter named Tanzin. She had married into a large merchant family in Manali and lived there most of the year. Later she gave birth to a daughter whom they called Oshin, named after the name of the heroine in a Japanese NHK television drama which was very popular in India.

Living with this family in Kardang was my first such research experience in the field of cultural anthropology. Since then I have lived with other Tibetan and Mongolian families for the same purpose. Naturally, there were comfortable households and uncomfortable households. From my experiences, uncomfortable households are those where family members don't get along well, while the warmest are the homes where there is harmony among the members of the house and particularly where the housewife is responsible. In such households the man may take the leading role in dealing with the outside world, but the actual power within the household is held by the housewife. I have felt quite comfortable in homes where the housewife was cheerful and managed her household responsibly. From that point of view, the Karpa family in Kardang were perfect. In retrospect, I was very fortunate to have found this household by chance.

Kardang is located on a narrow riverbank, similar to the other villages in Lahul. The rocky summit that towers above the village is called Dilburi, a sacred mountain for Tibetan Buddhist. A road for pilgrims was built around the rocky mountain, and during the summer the local people and many other Tibetans visit it. There are steep passes to ascend and descend along the way, and it takes a whole day to circumnavigate the mountain. During the summer season the soft grasslands spread under the rocky summit and alpine flowers bloom in profusion. Among the rocks one can find blue poppies, a celebrated flower of the Himalayas.

Tulshik Ngawang Namgyal (khrul zhig ngag dbang rnam rgyal: 1717-94), a monk from Zanskar, once wrote this prayer when he made a pilgrimage to Dilburi with his two disciples.

Glory to the great guru Chakrasamvara. Honorable King, the Dharma-kaya itself. The sacred land Dorje Dilburi. Noble Kolo Demchog, the compassionate protector. The same being as the great Dorje Chang. Here, two practitioners and I worship at your feet. Please bestow your blessings upon us. May the disciples achieve the same level of success as their master! Oh, glorious, clean and pure sacred land. Joy overflows through the beautiful and peaceful grassland in front of the mountain. It is clear all around Dilburi. Likewise our hearts are clear, without attachment, and free. By virtue of the Supreme Being, our hearts are joyous and serene. May we, blessed practitioners, receive the fortune of complete perfection!

Above the village is a small monastery belonging to the Dukpa Kagyu ('brug pa bka' brgyud) school of Tibetan Buddhism. Approximately thirty monks and nuns live there, all from neighbouring villages such as Kardang.

During the summer months, lush green fields spread out from the waterway that runs alongside the monastery. The waterway meanders through the valley and provides irrigation water from melted snow. In Kardang, waterways are drawn to the upper part of the village from two valleys located to the east and west, and the fields of each household are irrigated by these. Kardang tends to suffer from a lack of water, so each household is able to irrigate its fields only about once a week.

The village itself lies below the monastery, surrounded by fields and willow trees. The houses are crowded onto the narrow terraces, and the paths between the houses are quite crooked. A special, and not unpleasant, scent created by the mixture of dried grass feed and livestock dung fills the village air. Returning to the village after a long absence, this scent makes me feel at home.

There is a small shrine located near the road that runs through the middle of the village called Jabjes Gompa. Jabjes corresponds to the Tibetan term *shabje* (zabs rjes), meaning 'footprint', and refers to the footprints of a saint imprinted in the rock, although this particular *shabje* is said to be an imprint of the knees and penis of an ascetic. The shrine is built around the sacred rock.

In front of the shrine is a small open space and at the end is the only water pool in the village. A willow tree was planted beside the pool, and its shade offers a great spot for socializing.

Houses in Lahul are flat-roofed and rectangular in shape, similar to houses in other Tibetan areas. The white plaster used for Tibetan houses is beautiful, but unfortunately it is not the custom to use this in Lahul; instead, mud mixed with cowdung is painted over the walls once a year. Recently, more houses have been plastered with concrete instead of mud, diminishing some of the beauty of the village.

Many houses are three-storeyed, but those of the Domba people (also called Gara or Lohar)[2] who are traditionally blacksmiths by trade, have two storeys. In general the houses are large, especially some of the homes of former landlords. Usually, animals are kept on the ground floor and storage rooms and bedrooms are located on the first floor. On the second floor is a living room that is also used as a kitchen (a large room called *shersa* is used in the summer, and a small room called *chakstob* is used in winters for protection against the bitter cold). If possible, a special room is set aside for Buddhist practice.

An iron stove[3] is installed in the middle of the living room, and a seat for the housewife is placed next to this. As was the case in traditional Japanese houses, each member of the household has his or her designated place within a room. The middle part of the wall opposite the entrance to the room is designated as the head of the household's seat. The next seat belongs to the guest of honour. Next, both sides along the wall are occupied by other male members of the household in order of generation and their ages. Finally, the lower sides are occupied by the women. In particular, women and those who joined the family by marriage and also children sit near the stove at the lower end. Usually nobody sits along the wall on the side of the entrance, but Domba will sit there and beat the drum during festive dinners.

A 30 sq cm box-shaped altar called a *Latho* is set up on the rooftop of the house, and the head of the household will use this to offer prayers to various gods by burning juniper leaves. The flat earthen roof is also a very good place for drying or threshing grain. I used to love gazing at the snowcapped mountains, blue sky, red sunset, or the magnificent starry night sky from the rooftop.

NOTES

1. '*Dilbu*' means bell, a sacred instrument used in esoteric Buddhism. '*Ri*' means mountain. Dilburi is a holy land for a revered entity of the esoteric Buddhist sect called Chakra Sambara, or Kolo Domba ('khor lo sdom pa) in the Tibetan language.
2. The origin of the word Domba may come from 'Dom', an untouchable caste in Hindu society, with the Tibetan suffix 'ba' that is used to address a person. 'Gara' means blacksmith in the Tibetan language. 'Lohar' also means blacksmith in the Hindi language.
3. Stoves, along with window glass and a technique for knitting socks, were brought into the area by the missionaries.

CHAPTER 3

Economy

AGRICULTURE AND PASTURAGE

The traditional livelihood in the village is agriculture and pasturage, and nearly all the families still make their living this way.

Normally the farming work starts in May, with breaking the ground right after the snow melts. The soil is ploughed using dzopos, the first generation hybrid of yak and cow, who pull the iron ploughs and fertilize the soil.

First, wheat and barley are sown in the fields, then potatoes are planted in June, and followed by buckwheat in July.

Since Lahul receives little rain in the summer season, irrigation using water from snowmelt is indispensable. For this purpose the village has channelled irrigation ditches from two valleys on the eastern and western sides. Two irrigation ditches merge above the village, then they separate and run to the right and left above the fields. The person whose turn it is to use the water, has to dam up the waterway each time and dig a ditch to his own field. Bringing water to every corner of a large field is a tremendous amount of work, and people often work until midnight under artificial light to control the water.

There are strict rules for using the irrigation ditches that relate to family property, so I will describe them in a little bit more detail here.

Currently 25 households[1] in Kardang work in agriculture. Each household inherited water rights from their ancestors as a part of their family property, and approximately two to four households per day use the water. The turn for water usage (called *chures*) comes around about once a week.

However, water usage differs a little bit between the first week and second week, so in reality 15 days makes one cycle. The following is an example:

Week/Day	Family name for water usage*	Percentage of water rights
Week One, Day One	Mias	0.5
	Tachiji	0.25
	Tamas	0.25
Week One, Day Two	Karpa (Dorje)	0.25
	Larje	0.25
	Timorpa	0.375
	Deskiji	0.125
Week One, Day Three	Dhangrapa	0.5
	Manepa (Dorje)	0.25
	Manepa (Kangyur)	0.25
Week One, Day Four	Kilepa (Dorje)	0.5
	Kilepa (Tashi)	0.5
Week One, Day Five	Kinchespa (Sonam)	0.5
	Kinchespa (Ulgyan)	0.25
	Ankyanchi	0.25
Week One, Day Six	Thologpa	0.5
	Toas	0.5
Week One, Day Seven	Yuas (Tuktan)	0.25
	Yuas (Gyalchen)	0.25
	Karpa (Norbu)	0.25

	Karpa (Tserin Palzom)	0.25
Week Two, Day One	Mias	0.5
	Domba (Share for four families)	0.5
Week Two, Day Two	Tamas	0.25
	Tachiji	0.25
	Karpa (Dorje)	0.25
	Larje	0.25
Week Two, Day Three	Timorpa	0.375
	Deskiji	0.125
	(*bakhu*)	0.5
	Five families receive water allocation.	
Week Two, Day Four	Dhangrapa	0.5
	Manepa (Dorje)	0.25
	Manepa (Kangyur)	0.25
Week Two, Day Five	Kilepa (Dorje)	0.5
	Kilepa (Tashi)	0.5
Week Two, Day Six	Kinchespa (Sonam)	0.5
	Kinchespa (Ulgyan)	0.25
	Ankyanchi	0.25
Week Two, Day Seven	Thologpa	0.5
	Toas	0.5
Week Two, Day Eight	Yuas (Tuktan)	0.25
	Yuas (Gyalchen)	0.25
	Karpa (Norbu)	0.25
	Karpa (Tserin Palzom)	0.25

Note: *Name of the head of household is noted in parentheses when multiple families have the same family name.

Water usage starts at 6 p.m. in the evening and continues until 6 p.m. the next evening. This 24-hour cycle is counted as one unit.

For example, if the family's share of the water rights is 0.5, then they can use the village's water exclusively for half a day, or 12 hours. Out of these 25 families, only seven families have 0.5 water rights. These are Mias, Dhangrapa, two families of Kilepa, Kinchespa (Sonam), Thologpa, and Toas.

These seven families are called *tsan ku pa* (whole family household) and have maintained ancestral water rights without splitting them up. Other families have a smaller share of water rights because their families have split up, so their water rights have also been divided accordingly.

The four Domba families whose only turn for the water watch (*chures*) comes on the first day of the second week—so they can use water only once in a fifteen-day period—traditionally make their living as blacksmiths. They are socially separated from other villagers and speak a different language (to be described later).

Furthermore, the *bakhu* that occurs on the third day of the second week is a special kind of allocation, and five families who especially need water share this half-day water right among themselves.

In recent years the potato has been a very important agricultural product cultivated in the fields. Potatoes were first brought here by the Moravian missionaries who were once stationed in Keylong. Native to South America, potatoes adapted well to the Himalayan climate and are recognized for their contribution to increased food production for the Sherpas in Nepal.

At present in Lahul, two kinds of potatoes are being cultivated. The older and smaller kind was probably introduced by the missionaries, and the larger kind was introduced in the 1970s. The tastier smaller kind is consumed as food and the larger kind is sold at market as seed potato.

Along with potatoes, the villagers currently produce green peas, hops, and carrots as their cash crops. The land's altitude (over 3000 m) has worked favourably for Lahul because of the seasonal gap between the harvest times of their crops and those of the Indian plains. Therefore, Lahul's crops can be sold on the market at comparatively higher prices. Also, Lahul is conveniently located near high population areas such as Delhi and Chandigarh.

During the summer season in Lahul, one can see numerous trucks arriving one after another, pouring out merchants who wish to purchase the various crops.

This successful introduction of cash crops has dramatically changed the culture of this previously subsistence agricultural economy. For example, now, people in Lahul purchase and consume large amounts of rice everyday, which cannot be grown there.

The diet of the poeple living in this village can be summarized as follows. Barley, wheat, and buckwheat were the staple foods before potatoes and rice became available. Barley is an especially important crop. It is roasted, popped, and then ground into flour, and is the major dietary staple in most Tibetan areas. Usually tea is added to this flour mix and kneaded together, but yoghurt, *chang* (home brew) or soup stock made with dry meat can also be added.

Roasted barley flour itself–generally called *tsampa* in Tibet and *yusi* in Kardang–is quite aromatic and not at all unsavory. However, kneaded roasted barley is similar in consistency and texture to unbaked bread dough, and is therefore difficult to swallow. Since I hate foods that stick in my throat, such as pumpkin and yam, when I had to eat the roasted barley flour for two straight weeks in Zanskar, north of Lahul, I got quite fed up after a while. However, roasted barley is a whole grain flour that is high in fibre and nutrition. In fact, although I scarcely ate vegetables or meat during those two weeks, I was in excellent health.

Aside from being kneaded and eaten, roasted barley is also used as a thickener for soups. Easy to cook and carry, it is ideal foodstuff for travellers. A long time ago, a Japanese monk Ekai Kawaguchi, who entered into Tibet secretly from Nepal, was sustained by this food througout his journey.

Wheat is the second most important food in the traditional diet. As a staple food, it is threshed, milled and then kneaded with a little bit of yoghurt. After being left standing overnight, it is shaped into 15-cm pancakes next morning and baked on top of a stove. This type of bread is called *ketkel*, which is sour in taste due to slight fermentation. Breakfast with the Karpa family mostly consisted of *ketkel* and sweet milk tea. The left over bread was kept in a basket and served at lunchtime.

Buckwheat is likewise milled and mixed loosely with water, then baked over a stove like pancakes. Unlike the sweet Japanese buckwheat, it is a bitter variant, and cultivated in the Himalayan region. However, the process of making it into pancakes brings out the exquisite flavour, and tastes delicious. Unfortunately, and to my disappointment, these pancakes are only baked on formal occasions.

Rice, barley and wheat are also used for brewing. The threshed grain is first boiled and cooled, then mixed with yeast, and stored in a jar with an equal amount of water. After being left in a jar for a week or longer, it is ready for drinking. This home-made brew is called *chang*. Although its alcoholic content is less than beer, it is quite tasty even to someone like myself who is not much of a drinker. At the Karpa home, only *chang* made from rice and barley is consumed. *Chang* made from wheat is further distilled into a lower grade of spirit.

The distilling mechanism for making this beverage involves heating the alcoholic content of *chang* in the large jar below so that it becomes volatile and rises up. As the vapour hits the cold container at the top, it condenses and the liquid flows out (see Fig. 1).

This spirit is called *ara*. The word 'alcohol' is undoubtedly of Arabian origin and travelled east along with the distilling technology. A distiller with nearly the same mechanism is prevalent in Mongolia and the resulting spirit is called *alhi*. However, there is no corresponding brew made of grain such as *chang* in Tibet, and *alhi* is made out of milk brew.

The flours, breads and brews described above are the principal uses of the various grains. Other vegetables that are cultivated include green peas, cabbages, greens, daikon radishes, and turnips. Daikon radishes and turnips are cut

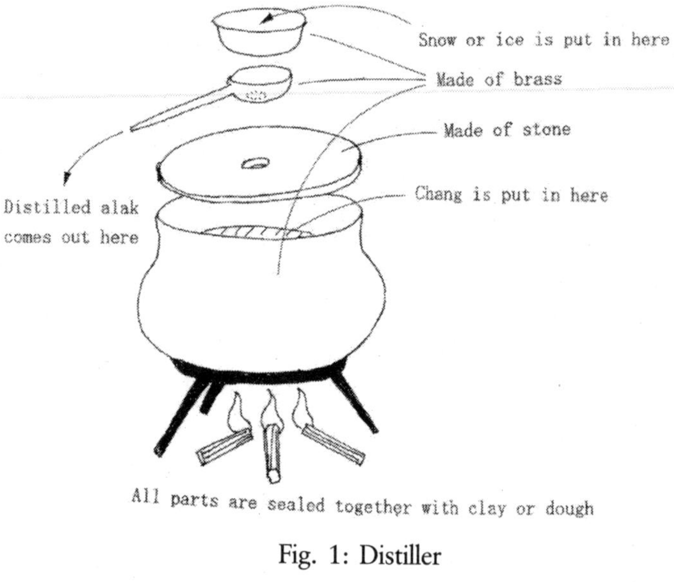

Fig. 1: Distiller

into small pieces, while beans and greens are dried whole, to be stored for winters. Dishes for ordinary meals are made up of these vegetables and boiled potatoes. In the late evenings or when it is very cold, they make a kind of dumpling soup (*thukpa*) with dried meat stock, dried vegetables and wheat dumplings. One can find *thukpa* anywhere in the Tibetan region as it is the most common dish.

On rare occasions, when fresh meat is available or when welcoming guests (such as when a monk is invited), they cook Tibetan dumplings (*momo*). This is done by first mixing minced goat or mutton with onions to make a stuffing. This is wrapped in cases made of wheat dough to make dumplings, which are then steamed or boiled. Momos are often prepared as a special treat in other Tibetan areas as well as in Mongolia.

Along with agriculture, stock farming is another pillar of people's livelihood in Lahul. Sheep, goats, dzopo and dzomo are kept by the villagers. Dzopo and dzomo are a first generation inter-species crossbreed between male yaks and cows; a dzopo is male and a dzomo is female. Because Lahul is not as cold as the Tibetan plateau, they raise more cows than yaks. In the case of Kardang, only one yak is raised communally for breeding purposes. The reason why they try to create a crossbreed of yak and cow is because that castrated dzopos are useful for tilling and dzomos produce richer milk than cows.

Strangely, it is not acceptable to eat the meat of cattle such as cows, yak, dzopo or dzomo anywhere in the Kardang region. So if a bull calf is born, it will eventually be left in the fields after being kept for a short time to encourage the mother cow to lactate. Sadly, the baby calf will eventually starve to death because it is too young to feed on grass. Adult cattle that die of an accident or natural causes are treated similarly: villagers pull a rope that is tied around the legs of the dead animal and throw it into a ravine. Such an action is unthinkable in the Tibetan dietary custom, where cattle meat such as yak is considered to be very tasty. I cannot explain with certainty the reason why they have developed such a practice, but the influence of Hindu customs on Lahul in recent times is quite evident.

Therefore, only goats or sheep are raised as livestock for meat. The blacksmith, the Domba, does the slaughtering. Meat is usually preserved as dried meat and used for soup stock and rarely eaten fresh. For the stock farmers, slaughtering livestock means reducing their capital, so there are fewer opportunities to eat a lot of meat than one might think.

Goat, sheep, cow and dzomo are all milked. The people drink some of the milk in their tea. The rest is warmed a little and some yoghurt is added afterwards. The mixture is then left for about half a day. With lactic fermentation, the milk turns into yoghurt. Yoghurt is then poured into a churner and churned for an hour. The fat is separated and taken out to use as butter. This fermented butter has a yoghurtish flavour that melts in the mouth and tastes delicious. For breakfast, one drop a piece of this butter into sweet milk tea and dip a piece of bread in the melted butter to eat.

The liquid that remains behind after the butter is removed is buttermilk, which still has a protein component. When this liquid is heated, the protein component starts to coagulate due to the heat and acid. The resulting solids are then strained in a sieve to drain out any liquid. These lumps, which are much like cottage cheese, are then shaped into small balls by hand and left to dry in the sun. They become so hard that it is difficult to bite into them and they never spoil. This is called *churpi* in Kardang and *chura* in Tibet and is quite different from the western cheese that we are used to eating. Its distinguishing feature is the use of lactic acid instead of rennet to coagulate the protein.

One can eat *churpi* by itself, but usually it is used as an ingredient in soups. It becomes somewhat softer when boiled, has a meat-like texture, and adds a good flavour to soups. After one gets used to *churpi* one starts to develop a taste for it. In the Tibetan capital Lhasa, there is a store that sells only *churpi*. It comes in different shapes, such as square pieces like caramels, or round pieces.

I will digress a little bit here. I once lived amongst nomadic people in Mongolia for about a month. I was extremely surprised to find that they can produce many foods from milk as if by magic. They use various techniques such as letting it stand, scooping and dropping it with a ladle, heating and churning, or boiling it down.

Compared with Mongolia, the Tibetan technique of processing milk in the Lahul region is quite simple. It is not necessarily productive to debate whether one ethnic group is agricultural or pastoral, and as in fact some Tibetan people are nomadic and depend solely on livestock for their living. However, the Tibetan people fall far behind the Mongolians in the organization of their nomadic lifestyles, with the aforementioned their sophisticated techniques of using milk, being one example.

Especially in Lahul, there is a reason for not being able to abandon agriculture and depend solely on stock farming. Specifically, it is difficult for them to store large amounts of feed for winter. Lahul is located at the southern edges of the Himalayas and gets significant amounts of snow. Unlike the Tibetan northern plains or Mongolia, in Lahul, if animals are put out to graze in the winter they will starve to death, because they will not able to eat the dry grass under the snow. Therefore, each household must cut grass from summer through fall in order to secure winter feed for the animals they keep indoors. Labour for grass cutting is limited, and the grass fields owned by each household are also strictly limited. To exaggerate somewhat, people cannot cut even a single blade of grass freely in the village. Therefore, the number of animals kept is automatically limited. In Kardang, the average number of domestic animals per household is a few cows and twenty sheep. This quantity can provide just enough milk and homespun yarn for the household.

Summarizing the common elements about traditional livelihoods such as agriculture and stock farming, it is difficult to expand upon their operational scale. For agriculture, the growing season is limited to just half a year due to the cold weather, the fields are narrow and situated on river terraces, and the water supply is limited. As explained above, expanding the stock farm operation is also difficult.

This particular difficulty at expanding their livelihoods, which is the basis of their society, and the nature of the zero-sum conditions define the Lahuli society, especially the structure of households and families, from the very foundation.

I will elaborate on these issues further.

NOTE

1. In 1987 the number of *kyum* in Kardang was 26. However, the Abiji family alone was not a part of the *chures* since they did not have their field near the Kardang area. Later, the Abiji family destroyed their house in Kardang and moved to the next village, Guazang.

CHAPTER 4

Household and Family

HOUSEHOLD (*KYUM*)

Currently, there are 26 households (*kyum*) in Kardang village. Just like the Japanese word *ie*, the word *kyum* refers not only to house itself but also to a conceptual entity that is handed down through generations and will be inherited by the descendants.

The household (*kyum*) and the family (*jinmad*, described later) are the two key concepts in understanding the social activities of the people of Lahul. In particular, the conflict between the two sometimes creates non-reconcilable dilemmas, and affects not only their activities, but also the emotional and spiritual lives of the villagers. In this chapter I will discuss various issues surrounding the conceptual framework of the 'household' *versus* the 'family', their conflicts and mediation methods, and gender issues within Kardang.

Each *kyum* in Kardang has its own name called '*kyum ming*'. For example, the name Manepa originates from being close to a pile of stones engraved with mantra (*mani*), and the name Larje (doctor) derives from the family profesion of physicians through successive generations; however, the origin of many names are lost to memory. The family with whom I stayed was called Karpa, which is their *kyum ming*.

A *kyum* operates as a unit to run village businesses. One member from each *kyum* (usually the head of the household) attends the village meetings. Matters such as water and pasture usage rights, workloads for watching domestic animals and maintaining the monastery are shared by each *kyum* unit. For example, the labour allocation for the maintenance and management of irrigation ditches is assigned according to the size of the usage rights of each *kyum*.

Within the 26 *kyum*, there are significant social differences between the four Domba families and the others.

Dombas are sometimes called Garas or Rohars, and the term traditionally refers to people who make their living as blacksmiths. This tendency to look down on this trade as an ignoble profession, and general discrimination toward blacksmiths can be found in central and western Tibet. What is unique about this in Lahul is that the Domba people there are also ethnically different from the rest of the villagers. Their chiselled faces and Indo-Aryan appearance clearly differentiates them from the Mongoloid villagers; also their language is said to be of Indo-Aryan origin. Domba people cannot marry other villagers, and although they participate in various events as musicians, they are not allowed to be official guests. Aside from working as blacksmiths, they also own some fields and engage in the slaughtering of domestic animals.

On the other hand, all *kyums* other than the Dombas are basically considered to be equal. The seating order at village meetings is based on age, and the style of administration is democratic. However, this means there is some potential for competitive relationships to develop among them. Competitive energy is focused on how well they achieve financial success and accumulate wealth into their own *kyum*.

Of course, there are older families with lineage in Lahul. For example, the Karpa family is descended from the family lineage of lords who used to govern the area. However, if the current financial condition of a *kyum* is not going well, other villagers will not value that *kyum* even if the family traditionally has a high status. The status of a *kyum* and the people who belong to it are interrelated, so if the status of the *kyum* is low, then the status of the people who belong to it is also considered low.

What Jiro Kawakita used to say about the Tibetan people of the Dolpo region could also be applicable here. That is, the people of Lahul rarely measure a person by inherent attributes such as family lineage, valueing instead, personal talent and ability.[1] The men under the *kyum's* patriarch will participate in various economic activities and accumulate wealth for their *kyum* to promote its status, and in return the status of the members of that *kyum* will also be raised.

There are numerous opportunities for each *kyum* to display its wealth in village social life. For example, it costs a significant amount to host a wedding ceremony, or a hair-cutting ceremony that celebrates the birth of a boy, with feasts extending over several days.

For example, there are two types of hair-cutting ceremony–one is called *lardacks* and the other *gotsi*. A *lardacks* ceremony is held for the first son of a married couple over a period of four or five days, most often during the summer. The host must prepare 500 bottles of distilled spirits and slaughter one sheep or goat. In 1987 it cost Rs.10,000 to host a *lardacks*; given that the annual income of the middle-class Karpa family was Rs.50,000, hosting a *lardacks* ceremony can represent a significant financial burden for a household like theirs. However, a *kyum* is not obligated to conduct a *lardacks* ceremony. On the other hand, a *gotsi* ceremony is held for all boys. It is held following the New Year day celebrations, and the feast lasts for a few days. Unlike the *lardacks* ceremony, the *gotsi* ceremony is obligatory and it cannot be avoided without becoming a target of criticism from other *kyum*.

Sometimes, a *kyum* will arrange for the complete collection of Buddhist Sutras (Kangyur) belonging to the monastery to be brought out and read at the *kyum*. On such an occasion, it takes around thirty to forty monks between five days to one week to accomplish the task. The cost of entertaining and offering alms to the monks can be enormous; Rs.30,000 to 40,000 may be needed.[2]

During the celebratory feast organized during a wedding or a hair-cutting ceremony, one unmarried woman of the *kyum* makes an appearance wearing many valuable ornaments that have been passed down through the successive *kyum*, called *changmo*. She goes around serving alcoholic drinks to welcome each guest. With her adornments full of precious Tibetan stones such as turquoise, gold and silver, the occasion offers an opportunity to display the *kyum's* wealth.

Such displays of wealth and entertainment are not linked directly to power. However, if a *kyum* is not capable of holding such a semi-obligatory feast, it is a disgrace to the *kyum* and may lead to some problems. For example, people may refuse to allow their daughters to marry a man from a poor *kyum*.

For the people of Lahul, it is desirable for a *kyum* to have many workers within their household to accumulate wealth, spend their money on holding splendid feasts and ceremonies, and gain appreciation from others around them in a proper manner. To achieve this, they need to prevent the division of their *kyum*. As stated previously, because Lahul's environment restricts the operational expansion of agriculture or livestock farming, it is practically impossible to double the operational scale of a *kyum* by dividing it into two parts. In general, there are probably no villagers who find it desirable to divide a *kyum*.

However, in reality the division of a *kyum* often occurs. A *kyum* that has not experienced any division, and kept its patrimonial family property intact, is called a *tsan-ku-pa* (whole household); a *kyum* that has been divided is called *phed-ku-pa* (half household). Of the 26 households in Kardang, only seven *kyums* are considered whole households. Indeed, they say that originally the number of *kyums* in the village was twelve.

Why did these divisions happen when nobody thinks a division is desirable?

In order to understand this phenomena we need to consider the power structure within the family, methods of inheriting family property, and the acknowledgement of parent-child relationships, etc.

FAMILY (*JINMAD*)

A family 'group' that corresponds to one *kyum* is known as a *jinmad*. As I will go on to explain, it is not necessarily appropriate to consider a *jinmad* simply as a 'group' as such.

One *kyum* has one *jinmad*. The Karpa family has the Karpa *jinmad*. A *jinmad* is usually recognized through the paternal line, meaning the line of fathers, sons and brothers. This includes male family members and their spouses, children and unmarried female family members. For example, in the Karpa family the couple Dorje and Palmo, their four sons, the wife of the eldest son and two grandchildren belong to one *jinmad*, but Dorje's daughter who married out of the family does not belong to the *jinmad*.

From among the male members of a *jinmad*, the *yonda*, the head of the *kyum*, is chosen according to his seniority of generation and age. The eldest man among the oldest generation in the *jinmad* often becomes the *yonda*, unless he is not fit for the responsibility due to physical weakness or other deficiencies. However, there is a condition attached to this rule. The *yonda* must be able to spend most of the year in the village to manage the *kyum* and its property. Because of this, a monk cannot become the *yonda* even though he may be the eldest member.

Unless they demand a division (*tsosis*), male members of a *jinmad* are considered members of the original *jinmad* no matter where they live. On the other hand, female members belong to their husbands' *jinmad* when they marry. If a woman does not marry out of her family, and instead brings in a husband from another *kyum*, then she remains in the original *kyum*.

As in the case of the *yonda*, the *yonda-mo* or the matron will be chosen from among the female members of the *jinmad* according to seniority of generation and age. Thus, the wife of the *yonda* does not always become the *yonda-mo*.

A *kyum's* operation revolves around the axis of these two pillars, the *yonda* and the *yonda-mo*.

Primarily, the *yonda* represents the *kyum* and participates in the village's business, and must negotiate with the other *yonda* for their mutual benefit. Additionally, and with respect to the internal affairs of the household, he manages the inherited family property, or depending on family circumstances, he makes appropriate investments and assigns other male members to take care of them. He is also responsible for making offerings to the various gods who protect the *kyum*.

Meanwhile, as assistant to the *yonda*, the *yonda-mo* is given the responsibility of managing the daily life in the *kyum*, and holds the authority to assign tasks to other women and younger people. In Lahul, most of the agricultural tasks are carried out by the women, but the *yonda-mo* stays home and takes care of the cooking and laundry. She has a seat right next to the iron stove that is used for both cooking and heating, and that seat is the symbol of her solid status. Other female members besides the *yonda-mo* who enter the family take lower ranking seats in the room.

Although membership in a *jinmad* is clear, it is not appropriate to describe the *jinmad* simply as a 'group', since *jinmad* members can remain in the *jinmad* yet have a completely separate residence and livelihood.

In Kardang, among the 78 male members over 25 years of age, only 41 are based within the village. Of the remaining 37 men, 8 are living away as monks and 29 actually make their living outside of the village.

The following case study illustrates the configuration of a *jinmad* belonging to a *kyum* in Kardang.

CASE STUDY 1

Chimed, Sonam, and Chowang are cousins and brothers but they share one wife, forming a polyandrous relationship. However, Tashi, Chimed, and Sonam make their living outside the village. Only Sharap, the *yonda*, and his son Chowang remain in the village.

Palmo, the common wife of these three men, lives with Sonam. Her daughter's father is believed to be Chowang, but Chowang dissolved his relationship with Palmo and took his own wife.

In general, the relationship between *jinmad* members who live outside the village and their *kyum* is delicate. In principle, profits gained through the *kyum's* capital are considered the common property of the *kyum* and should

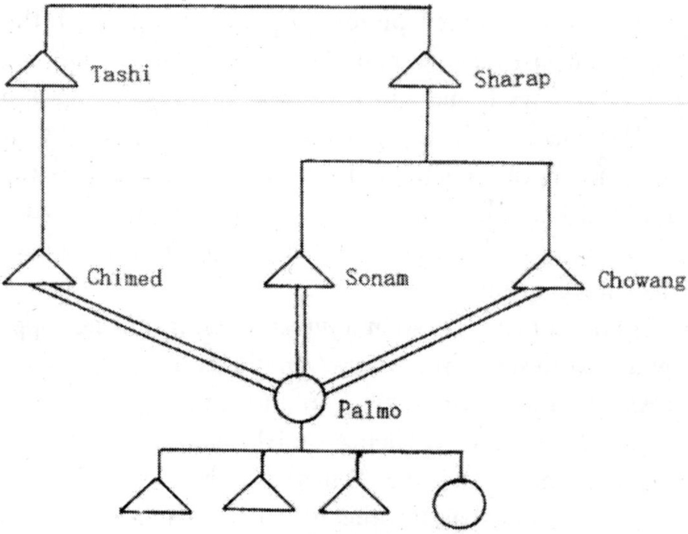

Case Study 1: The configuration of a *jinmad*

be entrusted to the head of the *kyum*, the *yonda*. On the other hand, any money a member earns from the government or a company as a salaried worker outside the village is considered his own. However, in the above example, while Tashi and Sonam operate stores outside the village and are well off, Chowang, who takes care of the fields and animals under the *yonda's* watch, is struggling financially.

Although one cannot generalize since each *kyum* has different circumstances, I assume that the only fund the *yonda* completely controls is the profit gained within the village, and that economic activities outside of the village are left to the discretion of each member in charge of those activities. While a military person from the village who used his retirement money for his own *kyum* was praised, the extent to which a member of the *jinmad* whose livelihood is based outside the village contributes to his own *kyum* may be a matter of personal ethics and discretions.

As a general rule, the male family members inherit the property of the *kyum*. This includes the patrimonial house, fields, stock animals, Buddhist articles, adornments, various tools and dishes, and usage rights for ditches and grass cutting fields. Also, as it has become a trend in recent years, for many *kyums* to operate stores or orchards outside the village, these assets are also included.

A woman who marries outside of the family does not have the right to inherit family property, but when she gets married she receives gifts of clothing, jewellery and money, and these become her personal assets.

After the father dies, the rights to the family property will be passed down equally to his sons. Therefore if there are three sons, each will receive one-third share of the rights. This principle also applies to polyandrous relationships, in which the mother determines the paternity of each child, and the child takes over his father's rights. In short, A's property will be taken over by A's son, and B's property will be taken over by B's son.[3]

In such cases, if the number of sons attributed to each husband is not even, then the proportion of inheritance rights will also be uneven. For example, if one of two husbands has three sons and the other has one son, then the difference between the size of the rights inherited between them becomes threefold. Also, if a husband does not have a son, then his status will be weakened. Therefore, certain arrangements are made for each husband in a polyandrous relationship to have an equal number of sons attributed to them.

The usual method of ensuring this is to designate the first son as the eldest husband's son, the second son as the second eldest husband's son, and so on. However, if a husband is absent for several years due to his job, the issue of designating an absent husband as the father of the child cannot be forced.

This allocation method is only applicable to boys, and there are no particular rules for designating fathers to the girls. In any event, by the age of six years, a child will know who his (or her) 'father' is going to be among the brothers. However, from the child's point of view, their father and his brothers (uncles) are all called *awa* and there is no difference between them.

The customs related to the identification of the father, the operation of the family property, and the inheritance of property in polyandrous relationships, differ widely in the various regions of the Indian Himalayan range, like Lahul, Spiti, Zanskar and Ladakh, that I have studied.

For example, in the village of Tino (25 households), which is located on the upper Bhaga River in the Lahul region, the same as Kardang, a father will retire when he becomes elderly, and the next head of the household (usually the eldest son) will take over the authority of the patriarch and the family property. The retired patriarch may operate a separate household called a *kangchung* (literally meaning 'small house'), but that is rare. Polyandry is frequently practised, and ten cases of it have been identified in the village of Tino.

In 1991, when I studied in Sani village (consisting of 30 households at the time) in the Zanskar region (north of Lahul, Jammu & Kashmir state), while polyandry was not practised as much, among a small number of cases all children were identified as the offspring of the eldest husband. In the village of Sani, property inheritance is equally distributed among the brothers, the same as in Kardang. On the other hand, the practice of the retired patriarch building a *kangchung* is very extensive, and out of 30 households, 19 of them had *kangchung*, and the total number of *kangchung* was 21.[4]

Furthermore, when I conducted interviews in Ki village in the Spiti region east of Lahul in 2000, I found that in principle only the eldest son inherits his own household and the rest of the sons will become monks or marry into other households.

The distance in a straight line from Kardang village to Tino village, also in Lahul, is only about 15 km, to Sani village in the Zanskar region is 100 km, and to Ki village it is also 100 km. Within the same land of Indian Himalaya and even in areas close to each other, each region has very different family configurations, marriage customs, and family standards.[5]

In Kardang, the distribution of family property can only be requested after the *yonda* dies, and once the division is decided, all of the patrimonial property and rights of the *kyum* will be divided strictly according to each share. On such occasions, people may encounter situations where they have to divide a cow, not land or money, into two to three portions. In such situations, they will determine the value of the cow according to the market price, such as Rs.5,000, and then the party who took the cow will pay the other Rs.2,000 or 3,000 accordingly.

In the case of water usage rights, for example, a half-day (12-hour) water usage right might be divided into six hours each, or each of the rights may be divided into four hours and eight hours respectively. Naturally, obligations related to water rights, such as the construction and maintenance of irrigation channels, will be divided accordingly.

Once the division has taken place, the newly formed *kyum* is highly independent and keeps its livelihood completely separate from the others. There are no family group relationships like the Head family and Branch family in Japan.

However, in many cases, the name of the *kyum*, or *kyum ming*, will remain the same after the division, and there will be multiple *kyums* who share the same name within the village. For example, in Kardang there are three Karpa households. When they need to be differentiated, the name of the *yonda* is added to the family name. So, our Karpa family is called Dorje Karpa.

The following case study describes a series of *kyum* divisions within the Tachiji family of Kardang that occurred during 1987-8.

CASE STUDY 2

Gyalchen, a brother of the Tachijies *yonda* Sharap, had a son from his late first wife and two sons from his second wife. After Gyalchen died his children asked Sharap for their share of the family properties, and they received one half of them according to the custom. (The rights of Sharap and Gyalchen were equal). But, because Tsering Dorje and Shama ran orchards in Kullu and lived separately, the house in Kardang where Sharap lived was not divided.

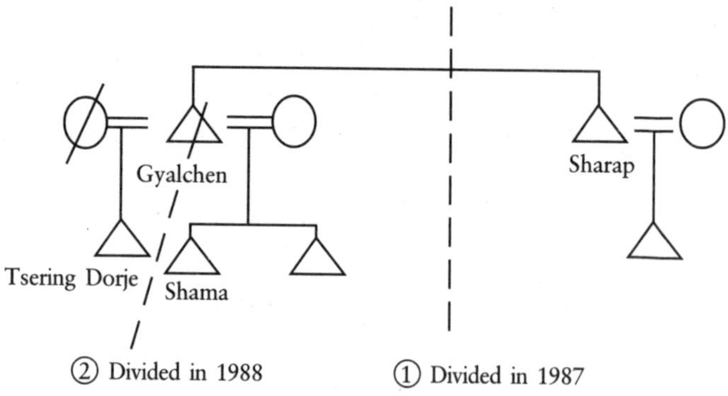

Case Study 2: The divisions within the Tachiji family

Then in 1988, another division took place among Gyalchen's children, who were from different mothers. Tsering Dorje took one part, while Shama and his brother took two parts of the family properties. According to a rumor among the villagers, the division in 1987 was caused by discord between Sharap and Tsering Dorje, but the reason for the division in 1988 is unknown. The final outcome is that Sharap, Shama, Tsering Dorje have divided the family property in the ratio of 3:2:1.

Since neither Shama nor Tsering Dorje based their livelihood in Kardang, another *kyum* rather than Sharap became the tenant farmers for the fields they own, and various obligations that arise from owning the fields also were delegated to the proxy *kyum*.

This Tachiji case illustrates the latest typical fragmentation of *kyum* in villages.

As described earlier, with the successful introduction of cash crops such as potatoes, significant revenues have been generated in Lahul in recent years. Villagers with capital started to seek investment opportunities, and they set their sights on running orchards in the Kullu Valley south of Lahul, or hotels and shops in Manali. Shrewd villagers from Lahul (as told in the Manali area) became successful at running these businesses, but also many other independent means of livelihood were generated within a *kyum*. Such situations encourage the trend toward fragmentation of the *kyum*, and those people who grew up outside the village have not formed an attachment to their *kyum* in Lahul.

Originally such investments were intended to increase *kyum* assets, but instead they have caused their fragmentation.

Problems surrounding the inheritance of family property are not unique to Tibet, but rather are common to all societies. In old Japanese agricultural villages, the question of how to pass down family wealth from generation to generation without diminishing it was a serious problem. A wealthier family might have been able to establish branch families, but otherwise only one son among the brothers, in most cases the eldest son, was able to inherit the family property. In some regions, it was even the custom to make the younger sons remain unmarried and stay in their parents' house for the rest of their lives.

The inheritance method practised in Kardang is the equal division among brothers, who can exercise their right to divide the property after the father's passing. One the other hand, the household, or *kyum*, is the foundation of the family, and it is desirable to maintain it without dividing it. Among the various concepts pertaining to household and family, *kyum* and *jinmad*, there are clearly contradictions.

Here, I shall call the *kyum* principle a symbolic space, where an entity for executing traditional rights and obligations and assuming a non-divided *kyum* under one *yonda* is a structural element of village life. On the contrary, I shall call the *jinmad* principle a conglomeration of family concepts, in which specific father-son relationships are recognized within polyandrous relationships, and the family property is inherited according to such specific relationships which may not correspond to other father-son relationship lineages within the *jinmad*.

The *kyum* principle is group oriented with respect to valuing the subordination of egos, emphasizing harmony, and maintaining a patrimonial household. In contrast, the *jinmad* principle is individual-oriented, as it allows for individual differences to be reflected in actions.

The problem of how to appease and reconcile two opposing principles, such as *jinmad* and *kyum*, or group orientation and individual orientation, becomes an issue on a variety of occasions in the village social life. Next I will look at issues related to marriage and the custom of obtaining a husband for one's daughter (*makpa*).

NOTES

1. Kawakita Jiro, 1970, p. 228.
2. For smaller events, gatherings for the recitation of scriptures are conducted by borrowing the village-owned scripture called the Yum or Doban.
3. Peter, who conducted research in 1938 in Keylong, across from Kardang, wrote that children were seen as the shared property of the household just like the land, so identifying their fathers was not an important issue. However, identifying the father of a child has had critical importance for the distribution of household wealth, especially for a boy. Since the current inheritance rules are considered to be the tradition, I have doubts about how accurate these writings of Peter (Peter, 1963, p. 325) are. The inheritance rules around the Kardang village area are almost identical to those of the Nyinba tribe (a Tibetan tribe that lives in north-western Nepal) that were reported by Levine. She considers these as being influenced by the Mitakshara system, the Hindu inheritance rules that are compatible with the traditional extended family system (Levine, 1988, p. 179).
4. Tanase Jiro, 1993c.
5. In particular, the case of Ki village is quite a contrast to the example of Kardang village, so let me elaborate. Ki village is located on the right shore of the Spiti River, on high land with an elevation of approximately 4,000 m, and the natural environment is rather severe compared with that of Kardang village. A monastery of the Gelug School called Ki Gompa stands on the north side of the village and about 200 monks belong to it. As of August 2001 the village population was 165; however, this number includes some monks and nuns who spend much of their time in the monastery. The number

of households is 31, and the average number of persons per household is about 5. This number is much smaller in comparison to the average of 8.5 persons per household in Kardang village. One reason for this is that in Ki village, parents frequently build themselves a retirement home (Kanchung) to live in as a separate household after the marriage of the eldest child, and another reason is that the custom of polyandry does not exist there, so many households consist of nuclear families. There are three endogamous classes such as Chozan (common people), Zo (blacksmiths) and Beta (musicians). The Zo and the Beta are not allowed to become monks. The concept of 'Bone and Flesh' that is so prevalent in Lahul does not exist at all in Ki village. However, the taboos against marriage between individuals who share the same paternal lineage are the same in these two villages. In the case of common people, only the eldest son may inherit the family lineage as a rule, and younger sons either become monks or *makpa.* According to a study on 14 groups of brothers who belong to the class of common people, 13 out of 14 eldest sons inherited the household and 1 left the family to become a *makpa.* All of the 14 second sons became monks, but later 7 of them returned to secular life. Out of 10 third sons, 5 were laymen (among them, 1 was *makpa*), and 5 became monks. Furthermore, out of 3 fourth sons, 2 were laymen and 1 was a Lama.

CHAPTER 5

Marriage and the Custom of Makpa

In 1987, one night after I had lived in the village for about a week, Ulgyan, the eldest son of the Karpa family where I was staying, told me that the people of the neighbouring village of Guazang planned to come the next day to kidnap a maiden. He even told me the approximate time of the proposed kidnapping.

The next day, the daughter of the Abiji family in the village, Rigjing-galmo, went to work in the field as usual, and there she was kidnapped by a merry party from Guazang, as planned. The girl was wrapped in a plainly made shawl and carried away to the next village like a piece of luggage.

Since this party would stop for a drink on the way back home, it took them a while to reach their destination. So when I arrived in Guazang ahead of them, I found that everything was completely ready for the party's arrival, with a large 'Welcome' written on a banner and small red and blue flags decorating the whole area.

In the house the feast was ready and the guests were already seated. Soon the 'bride', wrapped in the shawl was carried in, and as the ceremony began she lay between her groom in his golden silk Tibetan attire and his best man. In contrast to the satisfied groom, the poor bride was dressed in her work clothes for one of the most important events in her life. Sobbing as she lay wrapped in the shawl used for the kidnapping, she did not even try to lift up her face.

Ignoring the crying bride, a daughter of the groom's family who was adorned with large quantities of ornaments started to serve liquor to the guests. Thus the feast that extends over two days had begun.

Later, I had several opportunities to observe this type of wedding in which the bride is kidnapped. The practice is called *kunmai bagston*, which means robbery wedding. Of course, it is not a real kidnapping against the girl's will, and there is a prior agreement.

In Lahul, marriage opportunities for men and women are sometimes arranged between families, but often a love relationship will grow into a marriage. In the village there is a custom for unmarried men to visit their lover secretly during the night. It is called *shun pa* (man of the night).

When an official marriage is under consideration, the family of the man asks a third party elder to negotiate. The old man brings a bottle of distilled spirit to the family of the girl, and if the negotiation is settled, they will open the bottle and drink it. If there is no settlement, he will take it back with him.

After the first visit, the family of the man will bring several more bottles of distilled spirits and a jar of home brew to the family of the girl for another conference, then the final agreement will be made.

After this second round of negotiation, the bride may be kidnapped at anytime. The bride herself may or may not know the actual time and day of the kidnapping.

I witnessed another case of kidnapping on 15 August, during the Indian Independence Day festivities, in the middle of a town in Keylong across the river from our village. A car drove up in front of me and one of the two girls who were just walking along was forced into the car and abducted. It was quite a rough kidnapping but people nearby were merely observing and laughing as if thinking 'Oh, there goes another one'. However, the girl who was left behind was enraged and threw a big stone toward the car as it sped away.

That day large crowds from the entire Lahul region were attracted to the various festivities and cultural programmes, street stall shops and food shops, so it must have provided a good opportunity for the kidnapping. I heard that several other girls were kidnapped that day. Indeed, women who are engaged must be on their guard every minute. However, in this case, it may have been preferable to be kidnapped while dressed up for the festival instead of going to one's own wedding in work clothes.

Of course, there are ways to have a wedding without a kidnapping. For such events, a feast will be served on the first day at the home of the bride's family, and then the wedding will move to the groom's side for three to four more days of feasting. This is called *chuji*.

Kunmai bagston, the robbery wedding, is more common than *chuji*, because it only requires two days of feasting and therefore costs less. Also, if there has been a death in the bride's family during the past year, that family needs to avoid hosting a feast so they may request a kidnap style wedding. That is exactly what happened to the wedding of Ulgyan, the eldest son of the Karpa family, and his wife Norpalzom.

Along with these practical reasons, a theatrical plot may play into the situation whereby, although the marriage is decided, the family of the bride is still hesitant about marrying her off and the family of the groom is forced into kidnapping.

Of course, a young girl of marriageable age is an important worker for the family, so marriage is indeed a significant economic blow for the family of the bride.

For weddings in Lahul, a Domba will marry only a fellow Domba, but among other people (*phalpa*, ordinary people), villagers marry other villagers. There has never been a case of marriage between a Domba and a non-Domba villager. Although marriage between ordinary people does not pose social class issues, there is the one rule that should never be violated. This rule originates from the concepts of 'bone' (*ruspa*) and 'flesh' (*sha*), which are commonly observed throughout the Tibetan cultural sphere.[1]

'Bone' and 'flesh' are both ideological qualities a child inherits from his parents. Every one of the villagers is made up of a specific 'bone' and 'flesh' combination. For example, the children of our Karpa family possess 'bone' called Kinugopa and 'flesh' called Higepa.

A child's 'bone' comes from their father's 'bone' and their 'flesh' comes from their mother's 'bone'. In the case of the Karpa family, because the father Dorje's 'bone' is Kinugopa, and the mother Palmo's 'bone' is Higepa, their children's 'bone-flesh' combination is Kinugopa-Higepa.

In Kardang, there are only six kinds of 'bone' and 'flesh', and the rule is that men or women with the same 'bone' must never marry, even if they are not related by blood. People with the same 'bone' are considered brothers and sisters, so a marriage between them would be an act of incest. If a man and woman realize that they share the same 'bone', they will call each other brother and sister, and even avoid any joke with sexual connotations. (In anthropology, such a relationship is called an avoidance relationship.)

Therefore, if an unmarried man and woman fall in love with each other but they share the same 'bone', theirs is a forbidden love. This may cause some inconvenience, but every villager seems to know who has what kind of 'bone', and they cannot even imagine that two people with the same 'bone' would become lovers.

One exception was a case in a village in the upper Bhaga River region, where there was said to be a marriage between two people who shared the same 'bone', that of the former lord. As a result, the 'bone' of the noble family was lost forever and that household now claims a different 'bone'.

Monogamy and polyandry are the most common forms of marriage relationship in Kardang. Polygyny, whereby a man marries more than one woman–as opposed to polyandry–is also tolerated but is quite rare. Only one case has been identified in Kardang. Even in this case, the two wives and their children live separately in Lahul and Manali, and in fact this marriage is considered to be somewhat illicit.

Polyandry is practised in 10 out of the 26 *kyums* in Kardang. If the village next to Kardang is included, 16 out of a total of 37 *kyums* practice polyandry, so this form of marriage is practised among nearly 40 per cent of the *kyum*.[2]

Usually, in polyandrous marriages, the wife of the eldest son is shared by his brothers sequentially. Sometimes a cousin within the same *jinmad* may participate, but even a real brother outside of the *jinmad* can never participate. There are also no cases in which an older brother shares the wife of a younger brother later on.

'Marriages' with the second son and the subsequent

sons do not require any ceremony or feast and are carried out as internal family agreements. On such occasions, the wife of the eldest son does not reject his younger brothers, at least in principle, and the decision of whether or not to share the wife is left to these younger brothers' discretion. There is no clear rule that proscribes who is going to sleep with the wife during the night; whoever goes to be with her will leave one of his belongings, such as a cap, outside the room.

Even with polyandry the children's father are clearly determined, as previously explained. However, when it comes to calling family members by kinship terms such as father, mother, sister, etc., the children do not distinguish between their father and his brothers (the uncles), regardless of the form of marriage. They are all called *awa.* Likewise, their own brothers and sisters are not distinguished from the children of thier father's brothers (the cousins).

As well, from the father's perspective, the name for his own son and his brother's son, or for his own daughter and his brother's daughter are the same, and his own wife and his brothers' wives are addressed in the same way.

In short, parent-child, aunt/uncle and niece/nephew relationships are not distinguished from each other by name. Although children who were born into polyandrous marriages know exactly who their own father is, they still call all of their mother's husbands *awa* and do not distinguish between their siblings with the same parents and siblings with different fathers. From the father's point of view, there are no differences in addressing his 'own' children and his nephews and nieces. In addition, the name for his brothers' wives and his own wife is also the same.

Part of kinship term system for Punam
(Kardang area)

Relationship to the person	Name
Father, father's brothers	*Awa* (Except the eldest brother is called *awa*, followed by *petse awa*, *bara awa*, *awa tsi*).
Mother, mother's sisters, father's brothers' wives	*Ama*
Brothers, male cousins	*Acho* (The eldest brother is called *acho*, the brothers or cousins who are older than oneself are called *cho-cho*, and brothers younger than oneself are addressed by their personal names)
Sisters, female cousins	*Ache* (The eldest sister is called *ache*, the sisters or cousins who are older than oneself are called *apu*, and sisters younger than oneself are addressed by their personal names)
Wife, brother's wife, cousin's wife	*Diksa*
Son, brother's son, cousin's son	*Butsa*

This kinship term system corresponds well with their practice of frequent polyandrous marriages and their family ideal of keeping unity and harmony between brothers.

In reality, the vertical father-son relationship carries significance, yet by emphasizing the horizontal bonding among brothers, they avoid the explicit manifestation of the father-son relationship within the family. It can be said that the principle of *kyum* conceals the principle of *jinmad*. The kinship term system conforms to the principle of *kyum*.

Polyandry is a form of marriage that symbolizes harmony among brothers and the integration of the *kyum*. This is because once one enters into a polyandrous relationship, the potential rights each brother possesses for the division of family property cannot be executed. In practice, the youngest brother sometimes drops out of the polyandrous marriage, but in such instances he has to confer with his brothers and needs their approval. In several cases in Kardang, men who had broken away from a polyandrous relationship often started a separate livelihood by dividing their *kyum*.

Therefore, the assertion by outsiders that polyandry is adopted as a means to avoid the division of family property is not wrong, but is easily misunderstood.

Villagers themselves admit that by not entering into a polyandrous marriage, and instead each brother taking his own wife, the possibility of family division tends to increase, because multiple couples co-exist within a *jinmad*. But abandoning one's right to divide family property and entering into a polyandrous relationship occur simultaneously, and the actual situation may be closer to the statement, 'By not dividing the family property, polyandrous marriage become possible'. Polyandry is chosen because it concords with their own idealized unity of the *kyum*.[3]

If one really think of it, the reason polyandrous marriage seems strange to us is because we have a fixed belief that marriage is supposed to be a sexual and social relationship between one man and one woman. To go a step further, there is an ideology that says marriage should be based on sacred 'love' between a man and a woman.

Polyandry is one option among many traditional forms of marriage in the Tibetan society, and people choose it because it is right for them.

Although polyandry is the ideal marital form for the unity of the *kyum*, monogamy (one husband and one wife) is practised more frequently. The following table shows what kind of marriage is practised among a group of 27 brothers (including brothers and cousins) who belong to the same *jinmad* in Kardang.

1. All brothers share one wife	4
2. Mixture of brothers who practice polyandry and who are single men	4
3. Mixture of polyandry and monogamy	4
4. Monogamy only	15

Among the current monogamous marriages, some of them used to form a polyandrous marriage but other brothers who shared the wife have passed away, or some of them still have the potential to become polyandrous. Overall, polyandry cannot be considered to be the main form of marriage. The reasons people choose monogamy are quite individual, and one cannot simplify them easily, but one reason could be that unmarried men and women are free to date. Therefore, even if the elder brother is already married, the younger brothers may not wish to be married to their sister-in-law and may want to marry their own lovers.

If a member within the *jinmad* makes a practical living outside of the village, then it is not easy to participate in polyandry. For this reason, with the current economic activities of the Lahul people spreading outside of the region, one can predict that the incidence of monogamy will increase.

Polyandry can be described as a group-oriented marriage form since it reflects the idea of the unity of the *kyum*. In contrast, monogamy can be described as an individual-oriented marriage form because it is based on the will of each individual, and can trigger the division of the *kyum*. In other words, the conflict between the *kyum* principle and the *jinmad* principle, or the conflict between group orientation and individual orientation within Lahuli society, is manifested as the conflict of marriage forms between polyandry and monogamy. The fact that polyandry is desirable whilst there are more cases of monogamy shows that the *kyum* principle does not always dominate over the *jinmad* principle.

This conflict between the *kyum* principle and the *jinmad* principle can also be seen in the issue of *makpa* (husband for one's daughter) that I will describe below.

OBTAINING A HUSBAND FOR ONE'S DAUGHTER (*MAKPA*)

The term *makpa* generally refers to the husband of one's daughter or niece, but it may also refer to any man who marries into the family, especially when there are no boys in the family who can inherit the *kyum*. In these cases, the *makpa's* 'bone'–*ruspa*–must be absolutely different from the daughter's *ruspa*. Also, any child they have will inherit his father's 'bone', therefore the family's ancestral 'bone' will be lost when a *makpa* joins the family.[4]

'Bone' in itself is an expression of paternal lineage, and the fact that the custom of *makpa* exists tells us that paternal lineage does not play an absolute role as a controlling principle for social order. If the paternal lineage were absolute, when there was no son who was a direct descendant, a young man with the same 'bone' from another *kyum* would be brought in as the successor, instead of handing this role to a daughter.[5]

When there is no son to be the heir, the *makpa* who entered the *kyum* as its successor may even become the *yonda*, or head of the household, when he becomes the eldest man of the oldest generation. However, the daughter, as the *kyum's* direct descendant, rather than the *makpa*, holds the right to the family property, and on rare occasions she may banish her *makpa* husband.

Introducing a *makpa* is a necessary measure for the continuation of the *kyum*, but on the other hand, allowing a son to marry and leave as a *makpa* to another *kyum* is considered undesirable. This is because the property of the *kyum* could be sapped when the *makpa* leaves for the other *kyum*. The following two cases illustrate the *makpa's* ambiguous position.

CASE STUDY 3

Yoga practitioner Kunga from the Abiji family was a colleague of the distinguished priest, Norbu, who re-established the Kardang monastery, and both used to study under Tuktan Syakya Siri in the Kham region of Tibet.[6]

Kunga was married off after his return to Lahul and fathered a girl. However, he did not have a boy, so he took in his disciple Sonam Tanjin as the *makpa*.

After Kunga passed away, a young grandson of another disciple Wangchen Dorje was discovered to be an incarnation of Kunga, but the Abiji family did not bring that child into the family, and he died when he was about ten years of age.

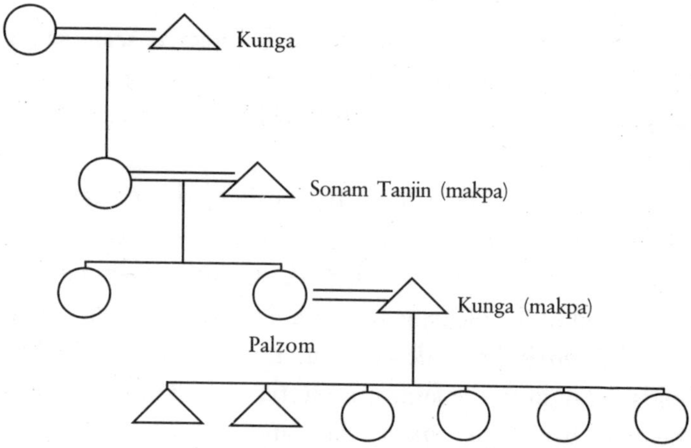

Case Study 3: Abiji

Since Sonam Tanjin who was the original *makpa* did not have a son either, another *makpa* was brought in from the Yuas family in Kardang for his daughter Palzom, and that young man's name was also Kunga. Palzom and Kunga had two sons and four daughters.

After Kunga (*makpa*) passed away, his two sons demanded that the Yuas family transfer the portion of family property rights their father Kunga had. Initially the Yuas family hesitated, but after several complications some money was paid to the Abiji family.

This case demonstrates a situation where a family took in a *makpa* for two consecutive generations, but it has a unique characteristic in that after Sonam Tanjin became the first generation *makpa*, the reincarnation (tulku: sprul sku) of his father-in-law Kunga appeared. Sonam Tanjin did not adopt that child because the reincarnated person is considered to be identical to the deceased Lama (in this case, Kunga), so his daughter Palzom could no longer be the legitimate successor of the *kyum,* and the very young reincarnation of her father could become the successor.

Usually the reincarnated individual is taken to a monastery and undergoes training to become a monk. However, if by some rare chance Kunga's reincarnation had chosen a secular life, Palzom and Sonam Tanjin would lose their right to succeed the Abiji family.

Also, the fact that the sons of Kunga, who was the second generation *makpa*, demanded the family property of the Yuas family–the *kyum* where Kunga originally came from–illustrates the ambiguous nature of *makpa*, as with the following case.

CASE STUDY 4

Among the five brothers of the Yankapa family in Guazang, one became a monk and the other four were in polyandrous relationships. Each of these married brothers had a son. However, the fourth brother Dorje moved out to the next village Kardang, and the fifth brother, Sharap, moved out to Manali, both as *makpa*. The family that Dorje married into was the Karpa family with whom I stayed in Kardang. Dorje fathered four sons and one daughter.

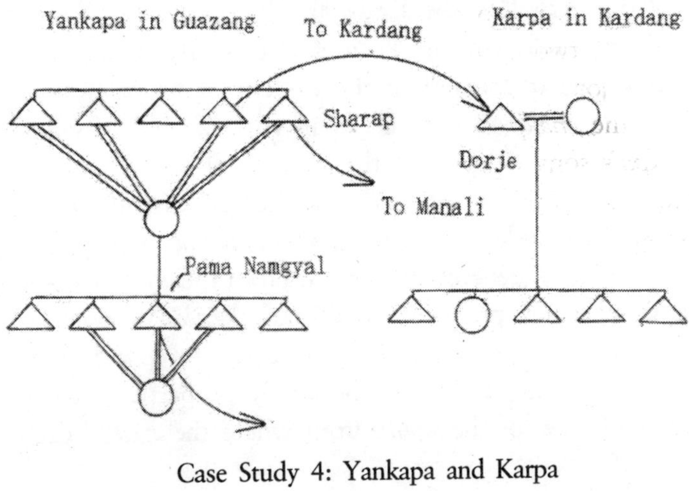

Case Study 4: Yankapa and Karpa

Meanwhile, in the Yankapa family in Guazang, three brothers among the five sons of Tsering Dolma formed a polyandrous relationship, but the second son who was said to be the son of Dorje moved out of the village and enrolled into the army and re-married (thus dissolving the polyandrous marriage).

In recent years, Dorje asked his family of origin, the Yankapa family, to transfer his share of the fields as his rightful inheritance. The Yankapa family did not respond to this demand and the dispute was brought before the court.

According to Dorje's claim, he has the right to one-fifth of the Yanpaka family property according to the custom. However, since he has one son (Pama Namgyal) on the Yankapa family side, and four sons (Ulgyan, etc.) on the Karpa family side, he thinks the Karpa *kyum* where he serves as the *yonda* can demand the share $1/5 \times 4/5$, which is $4/25$ of the Yankapa fields.

In the end, negotiations between the Yankapa family and the Karpa family were concluded, and half of Dorje's share, that is to say $1/5 \times 1/2 = 1/10$ of the Yankapa field, was transferred to the Karpa family.

These two cases are both examples of a *kyum* that a *makpa* joined demanding the cession of property rights from the *makpa's* original family. In the first case, the *makpa's* sons demanded the cession of family property after the *makpa's* death, and in the second case, the *makpa* himself demanded the cession of family property.

Both cases generated disputes. From the *makpa's* point of view, family property should be inherited through the father-son lineage, and moving to another *kyum* does not negate the right to inherit the family property. From the point of view of the *kyum* from where the *makpa* came, when the *makpa* leaves the original *kyum* he loses his right to inherit the family property.

The fact that these two cases developed into disputes illustrates that there is no clear rule regarding a *makpa's* inheritance rights to his own family property.

Even so, the original families of the *makpas*, in both cases, approved partial rights to the *makpa* of the family property in the end. In these situations, one can say that the principle of *jinmad*, which supports succession of family property through patriarchal lineage, supersedes the principle of *kyum*, that is, the ideal of unity among the *kyum* members and the common ownership of family property.

As illustrated in the second case of Dorje and Pama Namgyal, the annulment of a polyandrous marriage itself is an anti-*kyum* action in the first place.

As we have seen, I have addressed the issues of marriage and *makpa* as situations where the collision of the *kyum* and *jinmad* principles become visible. The principles of *kyum* and *jinmad* are both sets of concepts exercised and accepted within the society. In other words, by following either of them, one's actions are chosen, the collective structure is determined, and the property is transferred accordingly.

However, the principle of *kyum* is mostly related to ideals and symbolism and it resists changes, therefore its nature is not temporal. Naturally, ideals and symbolism must remain constant regardless of changes in the circumstances of the people who uphold them.

On other hand, the principle of *jinmad* mostly has to do with the rights and obligations of group members, and as such it can become a strategic tool for realizing one's individual desires. For these reasons, it potentially becomes a trigger point for demolishing a fixed means of group existence. In that sense, it enables changes in the group and therefore has a temporal nature.

To summarize, conflicts between the *kyum* principle and the *jinmad* principles, which create a distinction between conceptual groups related to family and kinship in the Kardang region, may be summarized as conflicts between group orientation and individual orientation. This contrast is expressed in forms of marriage as polyandry *versus* monogamy.

As for the context of both conceptual groups, the former has to do mostly with ideals and symbolism, and the latter has to do mostly with personal actions.

These opposing concepts can also be expressed as one with a non-temporal nature *versus* one with a temporal nature, or one that resists change *versus* one that facilitates change.

The following table illustrates the above-mentioned contrasts between the *kyum* principle and *jinmad* principles.

Table 1

	Kyum Principle	*Jinmad* Principle
(Marriage type)	Polyandry	Monogamy
(Orientation)	Group orientation	Individual orientation
(Temporality)	Non-temporal	Temporal

An ideal or a symbol, and something that resists change, is necessarily damaged by reality. The more it plays a central principle in society, the more urgently the damage needs to be compensated.

In the case at Lahul, the *kyum* principle is threatened and damaged by the division of the *kyum* itself. This damage seems to be compensated for by transferring the conflict between the *kyum* principle and the *jinmad* principle into a conflict involving the equation between 'Male' *versus* 'Female', and furthermore, by connoting negative attributes to 'Female'. I will elaborate on this point in the next chapter.

NOTES

1. Refer to Kawakita (1966, pp. 13–15). For the multiplicity of meanings that the concept of *ruspa* includes, refer to Levine (1981). Some point out that some of the *ruspa* in the Kardang village correspond to specific clans within Hindu society. For example, a *ruspa* named Darpanyanza is said to be same as the Katoch, the royal clan of Kangra. Also, people in the downstream region of Bhaga Valley, Punam, and the upstream region, Tod, use different languages, but most of them share the same *ruspa*.
2. Answering questions posed by Peter who visited Lahul in 1938, the then chief Thakur Pratap Singh told him that two-thirds of the households in the Keylong area were practicing polyandry (Peter, 1963, p. 314).
3. A seemingly simple question, 'Why do Tibetan people practise polyandry?' actually poses two separate questions. One is 'How did the custom of polyandry originate?' and the other is 'What motivates Tibetan people to practise polyandry?' The latter question has been addressed in this book. For the former question, many explanations have been given in the past. For example, Yamaguchi proposed a hypothesis that the origin of polyandry is the result of a compromise between the matriliniality and patriarchy in Tibet in the past (Yamaguchi, 1987, pp. 112–18).

   Peter sought the reasons for polyandry in their severe environment. According to him, for people who live in an extremely difficult environment, especially for brothers, "a tight unity among the male members is needed and this custom helps suppress jealousy. Their incestuous desires are fulfilled by allowing sexual contact with sisters-in-law, or in some cases, mothers-in-law. . . . Polyandry is a potentially homosexual and incestuous marriage system, and if there is no prohibitive rule against polyandry, it may have to do with the excessive economical and social burden on the structure of nuclear families who live under an especially severe natural and social environment' (Peter, 1963, pp. 568–9). I do not see any particular merit in seeking an original cause of polyandry. Once departing from the ethnocentric view (Peter's description is a typical example) that categorizes polyandry as a strange custom, questioning 'Why does polyandry exist in Tibet?' is as irreverent as questioning 'Why does polyandry not exist in Japan?' I wonder if anyone could give a convincing answer to the latter question.

4. Kawakita, 1966, p. 13.
5. There are no clear groups formed by paternal lines (called clans or lineage in anthropology) in Lahul. This leads one to believe that the paternal principle is not a dominant element in the Lahuli society. In general, Tibetan society is considered to be a patrilinial society. Certainly, considering the existence of the concepts of 'bone' and 'flesh', the fact that customarily a household's residence is in the paternal side, and that most of the family wealth is inherited only through their sons, these elements indicate that the patrilinial principle is a dominant factor. However, recent studies on Tibetan society tend to point out that the concept of 'household' is much more important than the patrilinial principle. For example, Aziz discusses the Tibetan society in Dingri near the Nepalese border in southern Tibet as follows: 'There is no ancestor cult, no clan land, no moiety marriage, no hereditary leadership and no lineage gatherings; all examples of social behaviour which would manifest itself where patriliny continued as an organizing principle are absent' (Aziz, 1978, p. 122). Meanwhile, 'the concept of household stands out as the keystone around which relations are articulated' (Aziz, 1978, p. 117).
6. Stutchbury, 1994, pp. 164–7.

CHAPTER 6

'Male' *versus* 'Female': On *Lettsoma*

While staying in Kardang, I was always extremely impressed with how hard the women work. Starting with milking in the early morning, then preparing food and doing laundry, they continue with making daily products like butter and cheese (*churpi*). Then, they go into the field to carry out all kinds of labour, even managing to draw water, cut grass and gather firewood.

Their work in the field includes carrying harvested potatoes in a bag to the collection station, that weighs close to 50 kg. Furthermore, as they chat with other women on their way to the fields, their hands are busy knitting socks and sweaters.

In fact, women are the main force in agricultural labour and all the men acknowledge that fact. Specifically, women are expected to form each *kyum's* own labour force. This is in contrast to the men, who may work outside their village. Even when the husband lives outside the village, the wife will stay and work within her *kyum* most of the year, or at least during the summer farming season.

In this manner, Lahuli society depends on female labour in everyday life, yet the villagers may attach quite negative connotations to the idea of the 'feminine' in some aspects of ideology and formality.

For example, most villagers nearly always cite the discord between *yonda-mo*, the elder matron, and younger women of the same generation as a cause for the division of a *kyum*. In particular, the conflicts among women who have married into a *kyum* are frequently very serious.

When asked why there is always conflict among women, and not among men, the villagers explain it as the fundamental nature of gender from an ethnological point of view. In other words, women are said to possess more jealousy (*jegdan*) than men.

According to an explanation provided by a monk, women possess seven times more desire than men. Therefore jealousies based on desire are far stronger among women. Also, women within a *kyum* do not want to be under the power of the *yonda* and *yonda-mo*, and they want to break up the *kyum*. The reason why polyandry is desirable is that it may prevent situations that encourage infighting between women of the same generation, and allows them to co-exist within the same *kyum*.

One curious thing here is that the emotion of jealousy (*jegdan*: zhe dang or zhe sdang) is identified as a threat to the value of a *kyum's* unity, as well as associated attribution of women.

Not only does jealousy sow discord among a *kyum's* members, but if it is abnormally strong, it can cause various kinds of harm to others while the person herself may not be aware of it. Women who unconsciously bring harm to others due to their extreme jealousy, are called *lettsoma* in Lahul's Bhaga Valley, and *dain* or *dein* in the Chandra-Bhaga Valley. In general, these women are found in every few villages, but are not called *lettsoma* to their face. Instead it is a rumor that is usually whispered behind their back.

According to a metaphor of the villagers, the extremely powerful jealousy of a *lettsoma* is like a large volume of water overflowing from a small container; it is uncontrollable and causes ill effects to others without the knowledge of the source. Since every human being possesses some jealousy, everyone has some elements of *lettsoma*. Tashi of the Karpa family was being quite cynical when he told me he thought every woman was a *lettsoma*.

In a way, the difference between a *lettsoma* and one who is not is quantitative rather than qualitative in nature. Some *lettsoma* lose their evil power after converting to Buddhism or getting old, due to such a reason. There is a male form of *lettsoma* called *gombo*, however, these individuals are very rare and a *gombo's* power tends to be relatively feeble. Personally I never have heard of any man labelled a *gombo*.

The damage caused by a *lettsoma* is varied. She may be blamed for cases of poor harvest or if a cow stops lactating, or perhaps even a stillbirth. In the latter scenario, the stillborn baby is called a *lettsoma-zaches*, meaning '*lettsoma's* food'.

A *lettsoma* is said to often enters into another woman's body, and the woman who hosts it becomes confused or starts eating ash. In order to dispel the *lettsoma*, the woman may be beaten, or a monk may perform an exorcism.

During such an event, the *lettsoma* (which is said to hide in the woman's ring finger) may reply to the questions of the monks or villagers and reveal her own identity through the hosting woman. The following example is about a woman who was actually called a *lettsoma* (the names are all fictitious):

CASE STUDY 5

Kyum A and *kyum* B used to be one *kyum*. Tashi and Kunga's fathers were practising polyandry. Tashi and Kunga did not practise polyandry and married separately, but they left their *kyum* undivided. Kunga and Dolma had two children, but the second son could not speak due to a mental disorder.

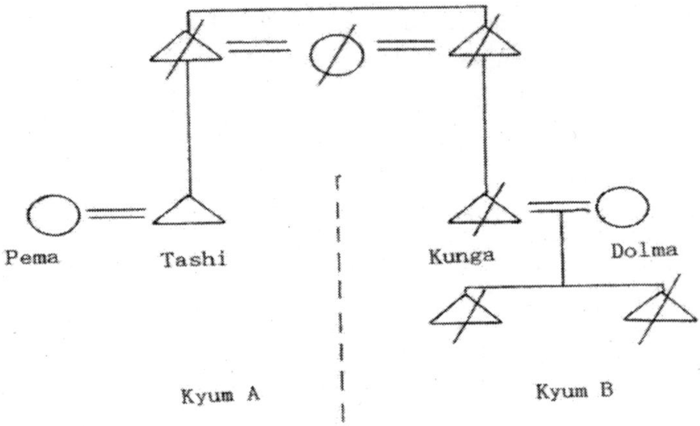

Case Study 5: *Lettsoma*

Almost 25 years ago, Kunga died when he was crushed under the tree he was cutting. After his death, the *kyum* was divided between Tashi and Dolma. However, later on, Dolma's eldest son died of an illness, and then in March when the snow was still deep, the second son went into the mountains and got lost. His dead body was discovered one month later.

According to the villager's interpretation, the family's continuous misfortune was caused by Dolma because she was a *lettsoma*. They believed that the division of the *kyum* between Tashi and Dolma was caused by Dolma's greedy and stubborn nature, and that the unfortunate turn of events proved that she was indeed a *lettsoma*. One time, a girl in the village was possessed by a *lettsoma*, who was said to be Dolma.

In the commonsense way of thinking, the domestic misfortunes Dolma suffered were not at all her fault, and therefore she deserves sympathy. However, a *lettsoma* harms people around her regardless of her own intentions because of her evil heart. That is why she is blamed for causing the family's misfortune.

As in the case of Dolma, most women who are called *lettsoma* are blamed for causing the *kyum's* division. But not every woman who causes a *kyum* to be divided or possesses a strong greed is called *lettsoma*. Some other reasons I do not understand seem to cause specific women to be labelled a *lettsoma*.

One interesting point is that many women from the old lord family line tend to be seen as a *lettsoma*, just as in the case of Dolma. For example, the mother who came from the lord family and her four daughters were all perceived to be *lettsoma*. This specific case illustrates how a woman may be called a *lettsoma* merely because of her family line, without taking her character into consideration.

Issues surrounding *lettsoma* are not just rumoured in a shrouded manner among the villagers. After the New Year ceremony of *halda*, between the 22nd and the 26th January in the Tibetan lunar calendar, it is said that *lettsomas* gather for their own feast. This is called *lettso-kunsu*, and large-scale exorcism ceremonies against *lettsoma* are conducted throughout the entire Lahul region during this period.

According to the villagers, between the 22nd and the 26th January, during the week of *lettso-kunsu*, *lettsoma* gather in a different location every year. However, on the 27th January they always gather at Karga, near the junction of the Chandra and Bhaga Rivers, and on the 28th January they gather at *lettso-ling* (place of *lettsoma*) within the Chandra-Bhaga Valley for a feast. There is a large boulder in Karga that *lettsoma* are said to jump over in order to see who is the most powerful.

During the *lettso-kunsu*, people place their sickles and axes at the entrance of their houses and attempt to prevent any *lettsoma* invasion by building a bonfire. Children throw into the snow a handloom (*kricha*), which is the *lettsoma's* vehicle, and a hard broom made out of aspen branches called a *shilpet* which is their weapon. Then they walk around shouting the following slogans in a singsong fashion:

Lettsoma! *Dangoma* (vernacular name for the female sexual organ)!
Wicked eye Woman! Monster! Evil Widow! Go away!
One foot on earth, another foot on sky.
Flame is flickering out of your mouth,
Smoke is trailing out of your nose. Go away!
Intestine as your sash, *koktsi* (rumen) as your towel,
Purpurtsi (reticulum) as your hat,
Kricha as your horse and *shilpet* as your whip,
Heart as your baby and liver as your hair ornament.
Go away!

During the *lettso-kunsu*, people sleep parallel to the ceiling beams at night because it is believed that the *lettsoma* will attack those who sleep perpendicular to the ceiling beams. Also during this period, monks will stay at the mansion of the previous lord, and pray to various protectors and local deities. In this way they gain a sort of supernatural power, and are able to identify the location of *lettsoma's* gatherings or missing items and predict the success of the year's harvest in their dreams.

These ideas surrounding *lettsoma*, seem to be largely influenced by Hindu as opposed to Tibetan culture.

Specifically, Hindu societies in northern India have widespread customs pertaining to the need to maintain large families and harmony among brothers. In these societies, women who have married into the families are frequently blamed for causing divisions, as well as being labelled and discriminated against as an evil doer who can bring harm to others merely by looking at them.

However, what is important here is not so much the origin of a certain idea or custom, but how conflicts between

Plate 1: Kardang Village

Plate 2: Dilburi, a secred Mountain

Plate 3: Women of Kardang Village

Plate 4: Lama of Kardang Monastery

Plate 5: 'Kidnap' ritual before marriage

Plate 6: Festival of Sadds

Plate 7: Terton Tulshuk Lingpa

Plate 8: Cham–Mask Dance

the *kyum* and *jinmad* principles, in another words, the conflict between group and individual orientation, or the conflict between temporal and non-temporal, is transferred to the conflict between 'male' and 'female'.

The reason why it is so important to note, is because the men are direct and legitimate descendants of a *kyum* whilst women are regarded as a potential source of discord in the *kyum* by coming in from the outside. One could say that men represent the *kyum* principle, whilst women represent the negative aspect of the *jinmad* principle that brings potential division into the *kyum*.

Adding the conflict between 'men' and 'women' to Table 1 depicted in Chapter 5 it looks like this.

Table 2

	Kyum principle/*Jinmad* principle
(Marriage type)	Polyandry/Monogamy
(Orientation)	Group orientation/Individual orientation
(Temporality)	Non-temporal/Temporal
(Gender)	Male/Female

Women, especially those who enter into a *kyum* through marriage, can pose a potential threat to the harmony of the *kyum*. This is because as women they naturally possess large amounts of destructive emotions of jealousy. *Lettsoma* is the manifestation of the emotion of jealousy, which is characterized the overtly grotesque manifestation of femininity.

During the *lettso-kunsu*, *lettsomas* are not only depicted as harmful beings who cause personal injury, but as a disturbing force that threatens the integrity and balance of the social order itself.

An example of this case in Lahul may provide an insight into the widely prevailing belief, not only in Tibet but in many societies, that the concept of 'female' is negative and women are seen as having a dangerous and defiling power.

The principles of *kyum* and *jinmad* were originally named as a convenient way of separating two sets of concepts operating within various ideologies regarding household and family in Lahul. However, at the same time, the conflicting nature of these two principles represents more objective contradictions about human nature, like the conflict between group orientation and individual orientation, and the temporal and the non-temporal.

Collective values and social symbolism are inevitably challenged and damaged, although by nature they regist change in the face of a continuously changing reality. It is quite common for specific values and symbolism to be abandoned because they are no longer suitable to the times and conditions, or to be destroyed by outside forces. Looking back at the modern history of Japan, one can easily list several such examples.

In the case of Lahul, with its various ideologies such as the literal idea of blood and flesh like 'bone' and 'flesh', or concepts surrounding the *kyum*, the more the value principles are rooted in the local lineage or blood lineage, the stronger the psychological and social resistance to changes must be. Ideology pertaining to men and women in Lahul may serve a certain ideological function to compensate for the inevitable failure to protect the *kyum* principle.

Of course, this was not fabricated intentionally. However, I believe that social and psychological conditions must have already existed for the concept of *lettsoma*, which was brought into society by contact with Hindu culture, to become established and develop into a significant ceremonial system. From this point of view, ceremonies of *lettso-*

kunsu can be understood as a social drama that depicts the crisis of social order and faith in its restoration.

In general, the conflict between the two poles of 'male' and 'female' is the most effective symbol that represents the contradictory nature of humanity. In fact, it has been reported in numerous societies that the conflict between the two genders is given corresponding meanings like 'sacred' *versus* 'vulgar' or 'cultured' *versus* 'wild'. Overall, these associations imply that women are lesser beings when compared with men and may even be perceived as dangerous.

These meanings attached to the conflict between the two genders do not remain in the symbolic realm. They support the actual discrimination against women with regards to the unequal distribution of wealth between the two genders, or the exploitation of labour, and various form of violence against women.

Many foreigners who have had contacts with Tibetan society mention the strong, cheerful and independent Tibetan women.

Indeed, many women in Kardang are also cheerful and strong and do not convey the darkness represented by words such as discrimination or oppression. But such observations are superficial and do not reflect the fact that women systematically experience structural and ideological discrimination.

At the beginning of Chapter 5, I described the episode of the Robbery wedding and depicted it as an old fashioned and quaint custom. However, it also could be seen as a formalized kind of violence against women, as could *lettso-kunsu.*

NOTE

1. Parry, 1979, pp. 164-71.

CHAPTER 7

Small Gods

The following incident happened during the second year I stayed in Kardang village, in the summer of 1989.

I was conducting a series of interviews about deities worshipped by each household, accompanied by Tashi of the Karpa family, with whom I was staying. However, he doggedly refused to accompany me to one household in particular. This was, according to him, because the local deity, called Apa, is an extremely dangerous being, one that frequently transforms itself into a giant, a cat, or a little girl, and prowls around the village menacing inhabitants. This particular family tried to escape from the deity, by moving their house to another location within the village, and worshipping another benign deity.

Because the deity was not given offerings anymore, it became angrier and harm people. It was alleged that at least two men in the village had died because of this deity. It was said that one of these men encountered the deity one night on his way back from the village doctor, and had died the next day.

The reason Tashi refused to accompany me was because he felt sorry for the people of the household who were worried about the dangerous local deity.

As I was listening to Tashi I felt a sudden darkness envelop my image of the village.

Until then, I had thought the deities worshipped at each household were only passively prayed to, or given offerings in a manner, similar to Buddha on a Buddhist altar, or God on a Shinto altar in Japanese households. But, these local deities here are not passively worshipped or regarded. They threaten the lives of villagers and may even cause death. It was hard for me to understand, but it was a serious matter for the household who worshipped the deity, and they had to move in order to escape from this dangerous god.

From that point onwards, I tried to pay more serious attention to people's stories, and I became aware of this supernatural dimension in Lahul full of various deities and spirits. This dimension sometimes grips the lives of villagers with a powerful force. This world, full of these small gods and bad spirits can be called an ethnic religion or folk belief, but it seems to be much more common and real to them than the world of Buddhist doctrines that every villager professes to believe.

Every house in Kardang has a square-shaped altar on the rooftop called a *latho*, on which the head of the household burns incense made of dried juniper leaves and offers prayers to the various protector spirits of the household. Also, when drinking *chang* or *ara*, villagers throw a few drops into the air as an offering to the gods.

The gods that are worshipped by each household may differ a little from each other, but they can be categorized into five basic forms as follows:

i. Yula (yul lha): Village god
ii. Sungma (srung ma): Protector god
iii. Fasla (pha lha): Patriarch god
iv. Jida (gzhi bdag): Local god
v. Sadd

The translations in parentheses are based on the original Tibetan meaning, but the villagers do not always agree about the characteristics of each god as described above.

I will elaborate on each of the gods in order.

YULA (VILLAGE GOD)

Yula is the common god worshipped by the entire village. In Kardang this god is called Yula Gandal, which refers to Tshepdamo (tshe bdag mo), the protector of the Gandal Gonpa that stands near the confluence point of the Chandra and Bhaga rivers. Although the Gandal Gonpa is now a very small shrine and no monks live there, it has been known as one of the most sacred spots in Lahul, along with the sacred mountain Dilburi that stands behind it. On New Year's Day and at opening ceremonies for irrigation channels, offerings are given to Tshepdamo.

SUNGMA (PROTECTOR GOD)

Sungma refers generally to gods who protect Buddhism. Ironically, many of them have a history of fighting against Padmasambhava (the great Tantric ascetic of the eighth century who brought esoteric Buddhist teachings into Tibet and became a mythical hero in Tibetan Buddhist stories). They were exorcised by him, and ordered to protect, rather than fight Buddhism. The Sungma in Kardang village include Palden Lamo (dpal ldan lha mo), Dorje Lakpa (rdo rje legs pa). They are gods with strange appearances who have gained their seats within the Buddhist pantheon.

In particular, line drawings of Dorje Lakpa carved on stones have been enshrined in many places in Lahul, and these usually become objects of worship called DoLa (short for Dorje Lakpa). Mounted on a goat, holding a hammer in his right hand and bellows in his left, he looks deeply pagan and folkloric. According to the scholar Nebesky Wojkowitz, Dorje Lakpa originates in Central Asia and has been worshipped as the protector of blacksmiths.[1]

Some households may have Jabtun Ngawang Namgyal (zhabs drung ngag dbang rnam rgyal) as their Sungma. Jabtun Ngawang Namgyal was not originally a god, but rather a Dharma raja of Bhutan with religious and political power, just like the Dalai Lama of Tibet; as well he established political power around the same period of time in history as the Dalai Lama. Also just like the Dalai Lama, he had been reincarnated generation after generation, but was expelled from Bhutan due to the political shift in the country during the twentieth century. The latest reincarnation now lives in Manali.

One reason why Jabtun Ngawang Namgyal is considered to be a Sungma, is because the Dukpa Kagyu School of Tibetan Buddhism of Bhutan has been flourishing in this area. Of course, when a Sungma is worshipped in one's house, the primary purpose of the god is to protect the house, not so much as to protect Buddhism.

A Sungma tends to walk around inside and outside of the mansion, and if his path is blocked it may cause harm to the family members. So, in the past, people used to drill holes in the walls, but now with glass windows it is not necessary to do so.

FASLA (PATRIARCH GOD)

Fasla are patriarchal ancestral gods. In Kardang, the gods called Fasla Motsi, Fasla Sersla, etc., are commonly enshrined.

If Fasla have been literally inherited through the patriarchal line, then they should correspond to the 'bone' (*ruspa*) which represents the patriarchal lineage. In other words, families with the same 'bone' should inherit the same Fasla. But, actual research indicates that the connection between specific Fasla and the 'bone' is not particularly clear.

This seems to be a result of frequent confusion between Jida, who are gods attached to the land, and Fasla. As I noted earlier, when a *makpa* (a man who marries into his wife's family) enters into a household (*kyum*), the ancestral 'bone' of the family is compelled to change. Therefore, in such cases, the proper Fasla of the *kyum* should be changed to reflect the change of the 'bone'. However, by treating Fasla as gods that belong to the land or the house, they often keep worshipping the same one despite the 'bone' having been changed.

In fact, in Kardang village about half of the households treat their Fasla as their Jida (local gods), these gods being attached to the land itself.

These Fasla do not possess dangerous characteristics like some of the Jida.

JIDA (LOCAL GOD)

Jida literally means 'the one who owns the land', and these are the local and domestic gods that are believed to possess real power. Jida in Kardang can be divided into two sorts. One has a strong territorial character and sometimes inflicts harm on people, while the other does not have a territorial character or dangerous nature, nor does it possess the original characteristics of Jida. These more benign Jida are mostly enshrined by households that have moved relatively recently to the village.

Some of the former Jida—those with original characteristics—are called Apa or Koteshin. The word 'Apa' itself refers to the grandmother, and to the female family members of the grandmother's generation, but Apa as a Jida refers to supernatural beings.

One trait of the Apa is that their residences are limited to specific locations, such as particular rocks or caves, or under the stupa (chorten: mchod rten).

Very few households have Apa as their Jida, but those who do, feel burdened by extreme troubles. As noted earlier, one household had to move away from their original place in order to escape from the dangerous Apa.

An old monk told me this story of his encounter with an Apa in his youth.

One evening, just as the sun was going down, I was walking alone near Pasporag (a village upstream from Kardang) when I met six young women in their 20s. These women were dark-skinned and not so pretty, but they invited me for a drink so I decided to stop by their house.

Surprisingly, their house was actually a cave, and inside I found a shabbily dressed old woman sitting down, who happened to be their mother. Thinking back later, I realized that she was an Apa. The old woman treated me with her home brew scooped up from a crock buried in the earth, and her daughters entertained me with their songs and dances.

Soon I got drunk and it became really late, so I decided to go home and two of the daughters volunteered to walk me home in the dark. I thought I was walking toward the village supported by the women on both sides, but I must have lost consciousness somewhere along the way. When I regained my senses, I discovered that I had been left alone on a mountain ridge. But it was close to dawn and I was somehow able to return to the village.[2]

Koteshin are the Jida for households with the lineage of the old lord family. According to a legend, a boy who was sacrificed when building the lord's mansion became this Jida. As with the Apa, this Jida also has a dangerous nature.

Unlike the Apa or Koteshin, Guatsangpa (rgod tshang pa) and Nyenchentangla (gnyan chen thang lha) are Jida without dangerous characteristics.

Guatsangpa was not originally a god, but was an ascetic of the Kagyu School of Tibetan Buddhism who was famous during the thirteenth century. Therefore, at first sight, it does not seem to make sense to consider Guatsangpa as a Jida, like Jabtun Ngawang Namgyal being considered a Sungma. However, Guatsangpa is also known for his magical powers, and the following legend is told in Kardang:

Once upon a time, Guatsangpa, who came from Tibet, was meditating in a cave. One morning, on the rooftop of the Lord's mansion below the mountain where Guatsangpa's cave was, a beautiful maiden was removing snow off the roof using a wooden shovel. However, the maiden dropped her shovel on the ground by mistake. Without hesitating, she stepped down on the ground with one foot while keeping the other on the roof, picked up the shovel and kept working on her task of removing the snow.

When Guatsangpa saw this he realized that she was not a human but a Dakini. He flew into the air and confronted the Dakini. She was frightened so she changed herself into a dove and fled to Kardang. In Kardang, she transformed herself into a rock to escape from Guat-sangpa's eyes.

Guatsangpa was able to tell that the rock was really the Dakini and he had sexual intercourse with her. Even now the rock is enshrined at the Jabjes Gompa, and the three cavities left on the rock are said to be the impression of his knees and penis.

Nyenchentangla was a famous mountain god of the Nyenchentangla range in Tibet and has been the object of worship throughout much of Tibet.

It is not known why or how Nyenchentangla became a Jida in Lahul, and even households that treat Nyenchentangla as their Jida are merely handing down his name without knowing his origin. From a strictly logical point of view, it is quite unnatural for them to take Nyenchentangla, a territorial god, as their Jida.

Older households tend to keep a Jida that belongs to a specific location, such as an Apa or Koteshin with their double characteristics. On the other hand, households that moved to the area relatively recently seem to keep a Jida who originates from historic characters, such as Guatsangpa, or one with a more universal nature (although within the Tibetan context), like Nyenchentangla. The latter Jida lack the ambivalent character of the original Jida and do not actively violate the reality of everyday life. As I wrote earlier, this is the main reason the household that moved away in order to escape the dangerous Jida took Guatsangpa as their new Jida.

SADD

Sadd refers to gods who have a beneficial influence on humans, and some people may include Yula or Fasla in this category. In general, the term refers to ten gods that reside within Lahul. Each of these gods has their own name. The two Sadds worshipped in Kardang are called Dabla and Tanjer.

Tanjer is enshrined in the village of Peukar upstream from Kardang, while Dabla is enshrined in the village of Piaso, next to Peukar. Tanjer is an especially well-known Sadd, and the following story is told about him.

Once upon a time in the Salan village of Tod (in the upstream area of the Bhaga River) where Tanjer was a sacred tree, a male was offered to the god as a human sacrifice. The sacrifice was offered by each family in turn, but one year it became the turn of a poor widow with only son. Her grief was especially deep but she could not refuse to offer her son and was helplessly waiting for the day to come.

One day, a Khampa came to her and offered to be sacrificed in place of her son in exchange for lodging and food. Of course, she was glad to entertain him as he wished.

But on the day of the sacrifice, instead of being sacrificed the man cut down Tanjer and threw it into the Bhaga River. Tanjer went downstream until it got stuck on a rock near Peukar, and the area became pitch dark for seven days.

Fearing Tanjer, the villagers of Peukar offered to pull it out of the river if Tanjer would accept a sheep instead of a human as a sacrifice. So, ever since then Tanjer has been enshrined in Peukar.

The rest of the Tanjer which was cut by Khampa (it is said to be a manifestation of the god) still remained in Salan, and in the old days sometimes Tanjer would visit Salan carried by men.

A very similar story was collected in the early twentieth century by Francke, a member of the Moravian Mission who stayed in the town of Keylong across the river from Kardang.[2]

Both stories tell how the brave action of an outsider broke the custom of human sacrifice, but according to Francke's version, the angry god drifted downstream to the Chandra Bhaga River until it reached the land called Kukti. In fact, even now the Keylong Devta (a Keylong god) is enshrined in Kukti.

Every other year the people carry Tanjer around to the neighbouring villages. The palanquin on which he sits, is the same as that of the other nine Sadds—a 20-foot long log wrapped tightly with many colourful pieces of cloth. A colourful rope is wrapped around the huge round head where a small silver canopy is inserted.

A small box called a *kyun* is attached at the tail end, but nobody is allowed to look inside it. According to one opinion, a fish-shaped piece of iron is placed inside the *kyun*, and if the portable shrine moves in a direction Tanjer does not want to go in, it suddenly becomes heavier. Only a person from the family lineage called *labda* can touch the tail end when the *kyun* is attached.

In the old days, a medium called *menba* made Tanjer possess him, and he spoke on behalf of the god. As soon as he uttered an incantation toward the sacrificial sheep, it was enough to make the sheep so weak that it appeared to be dead. In recent years, an offering made of roasted barley instead of live sheep is sacrificed for Tanjer. This may have to do with the absence of *menba*, or monks admonishing villagers for the killing of animals.

In the same manner as Tanjer, there are ten Sadds altogether that are carried on palanquins within the Chandra and Bhaga Valleys. Among them, Gepan is worshipped as the most powerful Sadd in the Lahul area.

Interestingly, Gepan and Tanjer are treated as brothers. According to one version, Zamlu, the Sadd of the Malana (in the Kullu region), is the eldest brother, Tanjer is the second brother, and Gepan is the third brother.

Malana is an isolated mountain village in the Kullu region, and the same linguistic line spoken in parts of the Lahul region is used there. The Kullu region is also known for its ongoing custom of worshipping a village god called Devta, who is also carried on a palanquin out of each village into the large festival ground once a year. Devta has mediums who express his will, and because of this, the Sadds in Lahul share more characteristics with the gods in the Kullu region to the south, than with those in Tibet.

The unveiling of Gepan, the most powerful of the Sadds, occurs every three years. He is carried by the people to visit a goddess in Udaipur in the Chandra-Bhaga Valley, and on some occasions he is taken over the pass to Manali to pay a visit to his brother Zamlu. Two people from each village in the Chandra Valley accompany this procession.

The unveiling of Gepan takes place in mid-to-late October after the harvest is completed. The speed of the procession is extremely slow, with the journey to Udaipur and back taking a whole month.

During this time, a sheep made of butter called a Mar Kyumtsa is offered as a sacrifice in the morning, and a live sheep is offered in the evening for Gepan.

On the second day of the unveiling of Gepan in the temple, all seven Sadds except Tanjer and Dabla of the Bhaga Valley pay their respects to Gepan by gathering at a place called the Gumtseling. After that, only Boti, the Sadd who is the wife of Gepan, continues to accompany him on the journey.

Surprisingly, in the Lahul region, Gepan is considered to be Gyalpo Gesar (rgyal po ge sar), the hero of the famous Tibetan epic, King Gesar himself.

In the fall of 1990, after going to see the gathering of Gepan and other Sadds at the Gumtseling, I missed the bus and could not get back to Kardang. By chance I met a kind man who offered to let me stay at his house for the night. After dinner, his grandmother told me the beginning part of the very long story of Gepan, who in fact is Gesar. According to her, it takes seven days and seven nights to tell the full story.

Once upon a time there were many demons in this world, and the suffering of the people was endless. The Supreme God of heaven felt the need to bring order to the world, so he decided to send one of his sons, Gesar, to live on earth. He prepared for this by sending his family members, Au Pali Gorpo and Meme Ganin Gonpo, in advance as Gesar's earthly father and grandfather.

The name of Gesar's heavenly mother was Ama Zandul, but a Rakshani (goddess) named Gogzal Lhamo was chosen to be his earthly mother.

Gogzal Lhamo was a weaver. One day while she was working on her weaving, a dark cloud suddenly appeared and seven hailstones fell on the loom and cut-off the threads in the loom. In a wild rage she grabbed these hailstones and swallowed them.

By swallowing the hailstones, she became pregnant, and seven children were borne nine months later. Because she was a virgin she felt ashamed, so she hid six children in a box and placed the last one into a stone mortar.

However, the rumor that Gogzal Lamo had given birth spread fast. Her young sister Maha Kaltinchomo became worried so one day she went to visit her elder sister to question her closely.

While she was there, she heard a song coming from the stone mortar:

'My mother's custom is to hide (the newborn baby) inside a stone mortar. Ordinary people's custom is to celebrate (the newborn baby) with *dadal* (a short stick tied with a white cloth)'.

When the surprised Maha Kaltinchomo opened the stone mortar, a little boy emerged. This child was the future King Gesar, who is also Gepan.

Gepan asked her to open the box where his brothers were hidden. When Maha Kaltinchomo opened the box, six children emerged. Four of the children held up *chapkyans* (a Tibetan kettle that is offered with tea or wine) and flew up to heaven, and two of the children remained on earth. These two children are Zamlu and Tanjer.

I was not only surprised to learn that Gepan was in fact Gesar, but was also greatly impressed by the good memory of the old lady and the manner of delivery. Everyone gathered around to listen to her story after dinner. Sometimes speaking quietly, whilst other times making everyone break into laughter, she was a masterful storyteller.

I have a Tibetan friend who escaped from the Kham region of eastern Tibet into India. He told me that in his homeland there was also an old talented storyteller with good Gesar tales. He said that on winter nights everyone would gather around him and listen to his stories all night long. At some points in the story, all the listeners were so overcome by emotion that they burst into tears.

As the Japanese folklorist Tsuneichi Miyamoto says somewhere, such master storytellers have been lost primarily due to the popularization of television in modern homes.

Television was not available when I first visited the Lahul area, but nowadays most families have one. Some households have even set-up parabolic antennas to receive satellite-broadcasting. In such households, they enjoy watching images on their television screens after dinner instead of listening to the stories of the elders.

I think about that night when everyone's eyes were shining with excitement in the dim light, as they listened captivated to the old woman's stories. I am aware of a sense of longing for such moments where I felt a love and a warmth towards all humanity. What a drastic contrast it is then, compared to be absentmindedly watching entertainment programmes of no value being broadcast from far away towns.

Gods of the Sadd group, like Gepan, seem to be related to tree worshipping. According to the lore, once upon a time Tanjer was a sacred tree. There is a great forest of juniper trees (*shukpa*) called Lhashuk behind the village of Tino in the upstream section of the Bhaga Valley, and in this forest are to be found the sacred trees called Gepan Buta, Yula Buta, and Fela Buta. Respectively, they mean Tree of Gepan, Tree of Yula (village god) and Tree of the Ancestor God. The leaves of the juniper tree are fragrant and are used as incense in Tibet. The older trees are twisted and warped into mysterious shapes and do indeed, look sublime.

Offerings are made to these sacred trees. For Gepan Buta, butter and a sacrificial sheep are offered, while for Yula Buta, along with sheep and butter, a cone-shaped mixture of tsampa and butter called *dange* is offered. For Fela Buta, only *dange* is offered.

The sacrificial sheep is killed during the ceremony that celebrates the arrival of spring, and blood from the heart is poured onto the roots of the Gepan Buta and Yula Buta. An altar is set-up in front of these two trees. It is adorned by the horn of a *kin* (ibex) and a white cloth called a *reka*, and leaves of *shukpa* are burned.

Grains are never offered to the tree of Gepan. The following story reveals the reason.

A long time ago, the brothers Gepan and Zamlu travelled together from the direction of Ladakh. They carried the seeds of grains in their walking sticks, but along the way they planted all of them except one barley seed that Gepan hid in his hat near Salchu (the farthest upstream point of the Bhaga River).

Zamlu travelled on from Lahul to Malana and Gepan remained in Lahul. The villagers asked Gepan to give them some seeds, but he lied and told them that he had none, even though he still had one barley seed left. That is why Gepan is offered only meat and butter even up to the present time.

Cutting trees in Lashuk forest is strictly prohibited. In addition, only men and children are allowed to enter the forest, with girls prohibited from setting foot into the forest after their first menstruation. If by some unlikely chance a woman steps into the forest by accident, wine and tsampa have to be offered in order to appease the god's wrath.

About 15 years ago a man tried to cut a branch off a dead juniper tree in the forest. He fell off the branch from a height of two metres and died instantly. The branch he tried to cut is still there, and the mark where he cut halfway into it still remains.

Each of the Sadds used to have their own mediums through whom they could speak their will. Indeed, the mediums for Gepan and Milan Tete Sadds were still living until quite recently. During the unveiling of Gepan in 1990, a medium was invited from Kullu who allowed himself to be possessed by Gepan and was able to speak his will.

The gods categorized and described above protect houses and villages. But there are also some dangerous evil spirits of the mountains and rivers, including the ones known as Tsan and Dud, who inhabit nearby mountains and valleys outside the villages.

There is, for example, a Tsan named Praktsi who lives in the valley near the village of Tino, upstream on the Bhaga River. Praktsi is also called the Red Tsan, differentiating him from the White Tsan, who lives nearby. The household that worships Praktsi places a red stone on its roof.

In March, villagers from Tino go to the valley where Praktsi is believed to live, and there they offer a cone-shaped offering called *serjon*, made of buckwheat flour and butter. After this, the spring grazing of livestock starts.

It is believed that Tsans roam around on their horses during the night. One can never see them, but may hear their footsteps. However, it is dangerous to encounter a Tsan. Often high fever, laziness, and nausea due to unknown causes—a condition called *dont pokches*—are believed to occur as a result of an encounter with Tsan.

Children are especially susceptible to *dont pokches* after they see red objects outdoors at night, such as skinned raw sheep meat. If this happens, they are cured by placing ash, buckwheat flour, butter, meat, and a knife on a plate which is circled over the fireplace in alternating clockwise and counterclockwise motions. This is repeated seven times in each direction, and then thrown outside everything except the knife.

A person's susceptibility to *dont pokches* depends on his or her disposition and age. A person who is more resilient to the condition is said to have *parka topo* (high *parka*), while a person who is easily vulnerable is said to have *parka mamo* (low *parka*). *Parka* originally means 'fortune' in Tibetan. In Tibet there is a concept similar to that of an 'unlucky year' in Japanese culture. In Tibet, for example, if a person's zodiac sign is the dragon, then every time the year of the dragon comes around, it is considered a 'critical year' for that person, and is also the year of *parka mamo* for him or her.

The image of Tsan is not consistent, and differs from person to person. But according to the stories I heard in a village near a tributary stream in the Chandra Bhaga Valley, Tsan looks like an ordinary monk from the front, but he has no back and his organs are open to view. The name Tsan comes from the sound of his wandering during the night, and it is said that if one hear the sound and become afraid, one will be susceptible to *dont pokches*.

Supernatural beings like the Tsan, whose influence is mostly harmful to people, are some time called Dud. A dangerous local Jida such as the Apa is sometimes considered to fall into the category of Duds. There is also a Dud named Kanrata, who may acting as a Lettsoma's agent and rape women to make them pregnant. Children born as a result of this act are deformed.

So far I have been summarizing various supernatural beings associated with the Lahul area, but when examining each individual element of their ethnological religious concepts, I found them to be interactive in nature. They may also be related to orthodox religious systems and great traditions; in this case, Buddhism and Tibetan culture. For example, in the Lahul area, they adopt the protector gods, of Buddhism as their own village gods and the house protectors, or Buddhist ascetics such as Guatsangpa, as their local gods. This seems to be the result of incorporating indigenous beliefs into elements of Buddhism. On the other hand, identifying the indigenous god, Sadd Gepan, as King Gesar himself can be interpreted as incorporating a great tradition into the indigenous folklore.

In reality, the various images and interpretations of supernatural beings differ from villager to villager. If there are a thousand people, then there will also be a thousand ideas about gods and spirits.

These ethnic religious ideas in the Lahul region are never fixed, and do not form a 'closed' conceptual system. They are still continuously interpreted and re-interpreted through interactions with the outside world, and as seen through the example of Lettsoma, also according to the group's internal needs.

Still, it is hard to comprehend reported incidents, like those involving a man who was said to be murdered by the local god Apa, or the man who claimed he was abandoned in the mountains after being entertained with some wine. It would easy to say that these were just wild figments of the imagination or illusions produced by collective fear. However, a world woven full of gods and spirits asserts real power over the people's fate and also the fate of their families.

Unfathomably deep darkness lurks throughout Lahul, in the deep valleys and forests, and even on roads and inside houses throughout the villages. The darkness in which Apa and Dud are rampant may only be accessible to the senses of the villagers who conduct their social relations within this profound symbolic world.

Such a world must also have been the kind of world in which our own not-so-distant ancestors lived, as vividly depicted in 'Tono Tale' by Kunio Yanagida. Modern society has erased the darkness and its inhabitants which were ever present in the world of our daily lives. But I wonder if the darkness of our hearts became even darker when that other world was lost.

NOTES

1. Nebesky-wojkowitz, 1993, pp. 154-9.
2. Francke, 1907.

CHAPTER 8

In Search of Beyul: Adventures of Terton Tulshuk Lingpa (gter ston brtul zhugs gling pa)

In the summer of 1961, a group were travelling from Lahul through Manali, Pathankot and Lucknow toward Darjeeling. The leader of the party that included over 100 Lahul natives was a Terton (gter ston: discoverer of the buried scripture) of the Ningma School of Tibetan Buddhism. His name was Terton Tulshuk Lingpa, from distant Amdo in Tibet. The purpose of this journey was to discover Demojong ('bras mo ljongs), a Beyul (sbas yul: hidden country) that was said to exist near the high mountain of Kanchenjunga.

Tulshuk Lingpa's party travelled through Darjeeling and then Kalimpong, and finally arrived at Tashiding in western Sikkim, where they stayed at the Tashiding Gonpa and the Sinun Gonpa until the fall of 1962. They stayed at Sinun Gonpa for about half a year, and in that place Tulshuk Lingpa performed the miracle of leaving footprints on a rock. According to one of the disciples, as he left his footprints, gemstones appeared from a rock nearby. Incidentally, these footprints are still enshrined in a small altar near Sinun Gonpa to this day.

During their sojourn in western Sikkim, rumours about Tulshuk Lingpa's search for the Beyul spread from Sikkim to Bhutan. Around the fall of 1962, many Sikkimese and Bhutanese gathered around Tulshuk Lingpa, and along with the people from Lahul, the party grew to around 300 people. At about the same time, the Sino-India border conflict had erupted, and the Indian army had suffered a heavy blow on the eastern front of the war.

In the winter of 1962, Tulshuk Lingpa returned to Darjeeling, and then he moved again towards Kanchenjunga, to the place of Yan Kuting in Nepalese territory. After half a year in Yan Kuting, he resided for one month at Tselam,[1] a location two days away on foot. Tulshuk Lingpa and some thirty people from his party left in the direction of the Beyul. However, due to bad weather they could not reach their destination, and were forced to remain in a cave for 21 days. When the weather improved, a rainbow appeared in the sky on the morning of their departure.

Carrying lighter loads, Tulshuk Lingpa's seven-member group, including his wife and senior disciples, took a shortcut. They stopped for a meal on the way and proceeded toward a mountain pass, but an avalanche crushed them just below the pass. Tulshuk Lingpa was killed instantly, and the others suffered serious injuries. In the meantime, the party who had taken another route remained unaware of the accident, and so they made a pilgrimage to nearby holy places and later returned.

Tulshuk Lingpa's remains were carried to Tselam where he was cremated. Tulshuk Lingpa died on 25 March of the Tibetan calendar in 1963, at approximately 50 years of age.

According to one disciple, a Lahuli who was with Tulshuk Lingpa until the last day, the reason why the search for Beyul failed was because the hearts of the members who accompanied Tulshuk Lingpa were not necessarily united. So the Sungma (Protector god) who guards Beyul caused the avalanche to drive them away.

The party lost their leader and all the members went back to their home countries. However, many of Tulshuk Lingpa's disciples have not lost their respect for their master. They built a large stupa to keep Tulshuk Lingpa's ashes, and a temple in the village of Teling in Lahul.

In this chapter, I want to explore the religious yearning that the Lahuli people continue to hold to this day, through the activities of the Ningma ascetic, Tulshuk Lingpa, and the search for Beyul he led.

THE LIFE OF TULSHUK LINGPA

Tulshuk Lingpa was born in 1916 at Serthar (gser thar) in the Golok (mgo log) region of Amdo (a mdo: the present-day Chinese state of Qinghai). His family had a nomadic livelihood and his father Kemchog Lingpa (skyes mchog gling pa) was also a Ningma ascetic.

After receiving a basic education in reading and writing at a nearby monastery, he entered into the famous monastery of the Ningma School, Katho Gonpa (ka' thog dgon pa) in the Derge (sde dge) region of Kham. At Katho Gonpa he received the teachings of Lonchen Nintig from the monastery abbot Ngawan Pelsan (ngag dbang dpal bzang) also called Pema Lerde Tse (pad ma las 'bral rtsal) (1879-1941). According to one of the disciples of Tulshuk Lingpa, Ngawan Pelsan suggested that he was a Terton, and so the name Tulshuk Lingpa was given to him. Incidentally, 'Tulshuk' means ascetic.

The Ningma School in particular has an extremely large number of Tertons. Their mission is to find the precious books and sacred relics that were written and hidden by the great saints, including Padmasambhava.

During the long history of the Ningma School, a large number of Tertons, both humble and famous, have appeared. For example, Padma Katang (pad ma bka' thang), the most common biography of Padmasambhava, the founder of the Ningma School and the one credited for bringing esoteric Buddhism into Tibet, was itself a buried scripture (*terma*) discovered by the Terton Ulgyan Lingpa (o rgyan gling pa). It was written by Yeshe Tsogyal (e shes mtsho rgyal), a consort of Padmasambhava, and in it fifty names of future Tertons are listed and their advent is prophesized.[2]

Buddhist scholars have pointed out that the Tertons in fact fabricated many scriptures of the Ningma School and lent authority to them by treating them as if they were written by past saints. They have been critical of the Tertons' activities by accusing them of taking advantage of the ignorance of ordinary people.

Zuiho Yamaguchi, for example, writes as follows:

> Originally, 'Buried Scriptures' were so named because Buddhist scriptures and documents of the Tufan Kingdom era were found buried in the sacred lands of that time, such as Samye, Jokang, and Tabuk of the Yarlung region, and were retrieved. But soon they started to deceive people by burying fabricated documents and then retrieving them in front of people. Slipping in a prophetic text among those documents and including a few suggestive lines about the one who is retrieving it (themselves), or acting according to already existing prophesies, their various actions have been frowned upon by prudent people, and the contents of the found scriptures have lost their reputation as well. In fact, numerous Tertons both great and small had emerged in this school alone. For this reason, genuine items are also subject to suspicion. One of the distinguishing features of this school is that so many aspects of it are questionable.[3]

We do not know when Tulshuk Lingpa left his homeland on his Terton mission. However, Tertons and yoga ascetics were travellers who made pilgrimages to sacred places, and many of them travelled all their life for ascetic training.

Tulshuk Lingpa's life must have been a continuous journey.

According to one theory, he left Tibet and came to India because Shunsep Jetsun Lochen (shug gseb rje btsung lo chen) (1865-1951), a female saint who lived in a monastery near Lhasa at the time, encouraged him to make a pilgrimage to the sacred site of Tso Pema (mtsho pad ma) on the outskirts of Mandi in Himachal Pradesh. Tso Pema ('Lotus Lake' in Tibetan), one of the greatest holy places of Tibetan Buddhism, is linked to the legend of Padmasambhava, who avoided being burnt alive by emerging from a lotus flower that appeared in the lake.

It is not clear when Tulshuk Lingpa arrived in India, but judging from the dates of the texts he wrote in the country, it must have been before 1939. He gained many followers among the local residents of the Lahul and Kullu region, and among Tibetans who lived in India (generally called Gyagar Khampa). Later, Tulshuk Lingpa's wife, children and parents left Tibet to settle in India.[4]

Everyone who had the chance to know Tulshuk Lingpa agreed that he had a profound religious learning, and at the same time, was a master of various disciplines including art, crafts, religious dance (Cham), divination, and medicine. Being a wandering ascetic, he must have had to respond to various needs of all kinds of people that he met on his travels. These skills must have been instrumental in helping him survive in his ascetic life.

When I saw a photograph of him, I was struck by his graceful and sharp features.

Aside from being a religious master, he was an expert in tracing the genealogy of reincarnations. He also penned a short text that records his previous lives. In this work, the genealogy of his reincarnations goes back to Kapina, an ancient king from south India who was led by Shakyamuni to become an *arhat*, and thereafter, eleven generations are listed before him.

Those eleven generations included Dawa Ngun She (grwa pa mngon shes can), a Terton predicted in Padma Katang, who retrieved the Four Medical Scriptures (rguyd bzi), the root scripture of Tibetan medicine, and Yuthog Yonten Gonpo (gyu thog yon tan mgon po), a famous medical expert.

Despite the prominent reincarnation genealogy that Tulshuk Lingpa displayed, in reality he never seemed to gain a significant position within the religious organization of the Ningma School. However, in India he received teachings from Dujom Lingpa (bdud 'joms gling pa), a leader of the Ningma School and a famous Terton himself, mainly about the buried scriptures. It is said that Tulshuk Lingpa went to seek Beyul because Dujom Lingpa encouraged him to do so. In addition, Jade Sanggye Dorje (bya bral sangs rgyas rdo rjes) was a Dharma friend of Tulshuk Lingpa, and his teacher was also Ngawan Pelsan. Later one of Tulshuk Lingpa's daughters became Jade Sangye Dorje's wife (sanyum).

THE TALE OF GERE LAMA

While he was in India, Tulshuk Lingpa stayed in Kullu during the winters. He spent his summers in Lahul, where he instructed people in the teachings of the Ningma School and increased his following. The scriptures and prayer texts he used were collected by his disciples and published after his death in a volume called *The Collected Revelations (gter chos) and Writings of brtul-zugs-gling-pa.*[5]

Among them is a text that describes a mysterious experience Tulshuk Lingpa had in Lahul, enlisted *A History of the Holy Place Gere Near Mayul Valley: The Lapis Lazuli Necklace* (chu bo me ya re'i 'gram klung gye re gnas kyi rnam bshad nor bu be tu'urya phreng ba bshugs so).[6] I wish to take this into consideration here because it is an interesting text that offers insight into Tulshuk Lingpa's activities as a Terton, and the strategy behind his charisma.

In order to make the account more readable, I have added a few words and changed some paragraphs from the original Tibetan text.

The Mayul Valley noted in the title is a tributary valley of the Chandra Bhaga River that runs through Lahul. The well-known white marble statue of Avalokitesvara in Thiloknath temple is one of the holy images that the Tibetan and Indian people make a point of seeing during their pilgrimage. There were many followers of Tulshuk Lingpa in the Mayul Valley, and his parents lived there until they died.

Chronologically, the text begins on 25 July 1954, when Tulshuk Lingpa received a sign from a golden Dakini who appeared in the middle of the sky while he was crossing the Mayul Valley.

'Oh, brave warrior, know the actions that the great saint Kumara Senha (Gere Lama) by which he opened anew the door of enlightenment!'[7]

At the time, one of the people who was accompanying Tulshuk Lingpa told him that, nearby, there was an old meditation hut used by a saint named Gere Lama, so the party proceeded towards it. There, they found a *shabje* of Gere Lama.

I (Tulshuk Lingpa) found a footprint of the Lama's right foot on the surface of a square rock near a wall, and realized that no one had noticed it until then. I deserved to make this discovery due to the actions of my previous lives.

At that moment, some of my disciples and attendants pulled out a huge rock with three cracks from the middle of the road. A tracing of the Lama's entire body could be clearly seen on its surface. Everyone confirmed that the mark was that of Gere Lama's body. We also found another rock nearby that had a mark of the Lama's pelvic region. So we placed all these rocks with marks of his body and pelvic region in the middle of the road, and thirteen of us, the master and his disciples, offered a mandala and flowers and prayed for it.

That night, while he stayed at his patron's house, the Dakini again appeared in Tulshuk Lingpa's dream. In the dream she began to tell a story about the origin of the *shabje* that the party of Tulshuk Lingpa had found during the day, and the murder of Gere Lama committed by Palden Sangmo, a daughter of the chief of those days.

The Dakini's tale reads:

In those days, Jobo Sonam Tobden, the chief of eighteen villages in the Gere region, had a daughter named Palden Sangmo who was very outspoken and possessed much wealth and many fields. Among these fields, the soil of a field called Pema Tang was of outstanding quality.

However, every year when the crops in the Pema Tang were ready for harvesting, Gere Lama always made his way across the field on his horse. Palden Sangmo was feeling bitter about his actions and became increasingly impatient, for his violations occurred too frequently.

When Palden Sangmo heard the news that Gere Lama would arrive next day, she gathered nine young men from the village and entertained them with meat and wine until they were amply satisfied. She said: 'Young men, please listen to me. From our tribe which lives in the Mayul Valley up to Thiloknath and Maruta, there is no one stronger and wealthier than Jobo Sonam Tobden. Yet we all have been paying our respects to Lama Syunnu Senge (Gere Lama). Nevertheless, no matter how much we worship him or give him offerings, he does not have any modesty. You all know how he goes back and forth in the Pema Tang field every year. Last year I threw a stone at him and asked him to go on the road rather than crossing my field. He replied, 'I will not go around the field. I will go through your field as long as I live.' Not only that, he shouted angrily at me, 'What would you do if I ran over your head with my horse?' When the Lama comes today, let's dig a huge hole at the edge of the Pema Tang, hide its opening by covering it with wooden branches, and throw the man and his horse into the hole and crush him with a huge rock.' She repeatedly enticed the young men to submit to her.'

Meanwhile, the local god Kunse warned Gere Lama of the danger but he did not heed the warning.

He replied, 'Oh, protector of the righteous ones, Kunse, I am well aware of this plot. This woman, Palden Sangmo, was a devil woman in her previous life. I dug a pitfall and murdered her by crushing her with a rock.

This revenge is desirable and not to be grieved. I have accomplished the task of enlightening people in a short period of time. It is not desirable to live any longer. I will not die inside the hole that was dug in the ground. I will not be crushed and hurt by the rock.

I have gained the power to master the Four Great elements (Earth, Water, Fire, and Wind that form the world). Life and death are both pure in such a state. And my task of enlightening others has been completed.

Being aware of the fate reserved to him, Gere Lama willingly fell into the pitfall.

So the horse fell into the pitfall dug at the edge of Pema Tang. After that, a rock fell in and hit the Lama's waist, but it did not hurt him. Instead, the rock miraculously yielded into a saddle shape, and Gere Lama threw the horse out of the opening of the hole.

However, another huge rock rolled into the hole and the body of Gere Lama was crushed under it. His entire body was pressed into the surface of the rock as if it were moulded into mud. Only the top of his head and his legs could be seen outside it. His body being badly crushed, blood filled the hole and covered the entire rock. Hot blood and body fluid soaked the rock and ran out in waves.

The story of the *shabje* found by Tulshuk Lingpa follows:

The gods and spirits gathered at once and cried violently, and Dakinis came from the sky. All the dwellers of the eighteen villages in the Gere region heard the mysterious sound of a conch shell, which they had never heard before. A tremendous fear arose in the heart of Palden Sangmo.

'Considering how musical sounds are filling the heaven and earth, numerous gods and protector spirits must be gathering for the death of the Lama and his horse. I wonder if something terrible could happen to my family, wealth and animals.' She worried so much that she could not sleep at all at night and felt as if she were going mad.

The next morning, villagers from the eighteen villages of the Gere region gathered and came to survey the condition of Pema Tang. Although both the Lama and his horse had fallen into the pitfall, the horse was standing outside it, eating grass nearby. As for the Lama, he was crushed under the rock and sunk in his own blood inside the hole. His head and legs could be seen. When the young men pulled out the rock, the Lama's body was pressed onto the rock so hard that they had to peel off his remains and lay them in state.

An elderly man suggested to Palden Sangmo, who had gone mad after realizing that Gere Lama was indeed a real saint, that, if she repented, she should respectfully perform a memorial service for him by building a stupa.

'You, lords, have a strong pride and lust for power, and do not try to notice virtue in others. We poor people knew that Lama Syunnu Senge was a virtuous man.

Every year from August through May, Lama Rinpoche used to carry one load of fuel and one load of food to 'the cave where dharma is born and burns brightly'. The cave is located upstream from this valley at the foot of the snowy Dukuten mountain, near the 'lake where melting turquoise returns' and above the 'palace of sixteen of Buddha's disciples who attained enlightenment'. There was only one set of cotton clothes and one piece of *kin* (ibex) skin there. The Lama led this simple lifestyle for the last 20 years and 5 months until this tragedy happened. This one thing alone indeed proves that he was a saint.

Needing to do so, he led his horse into your Pema Tang field, and you were consumed by anger.

However, because he was a great Bodhisattva, he did not entice protector gods for revenge because he cared about you. In spite of this, you did something irreparable. Now, if you really grieve, regret and fear what your have done, you need to accumulate good deeds, such as building a stupa.'

Judging from this account, I cannot avoid thinking that Tulshuk Lingpa's attitude could have been projected onto the Gere Lama. As a stranger from Tibet and a Ningma ascetic who marries and drinks, Tulshuk Lingpa could have been frowned upon in Lahul. In fact, there are few followers of Tulshuk Lingpa in the area downstream on the Bhaga River (Punam) where Kardang Gompa, a Kagyu monastery, is still situated, within the Lahul area.

It is possible that many people in Lahul considered Tulshuk Lingpa to be quite a disreputable character. In order to gain followers in such an environment, he needed to produce some miracles. He was not always successful. Dorje of the Karpa family where I was boarding remembered that Tulshuk Lingpa, despite having been commissioned to do so, failed to make rainfall after performing a ritual.

Returning the story, another miracle happened when all of the nearby residents gathered to witness the beginning of the impressive funeral ceremony for Gere Lama. From the flame that was cremating Gere Lama's body, a boy of around eight years old with the appearance of a monk emerged, and said that Buddhism should be valued:

Palden Sangmo and everyone who has gathered here should listen well. Always pay respect to all Lamas who follow Buddhism, and abandon your wrong views. Value noble thoughts and always depend on them; shake off ignorance and seek Dharma.

Human birth is a purposeful and precious opportunity. Death is an unavoidable divine law. Think of the suffering of repeated reincarnations in the six worlds. Karma depends on your discipline and diligence.

Monks are the feet of Dharma. Aspiration for enlightenment is the body of Dharma. Clear thought is the head of Dharma. The meaning of the three precepts essentially boils down to this. Make an effort and do not say you have no opportunity. Surrender attachment, hatred and the eight worldly objects. Cut out jealousy, which is the root of the five addictions. Renounce the trivial things in life. Seek pure Dharma immediately. Always take refuge in the Three Jewels. Correct your sins and mistakes by means of clear thoughts: this will increase your good fortune and happiness. Give up your doubts and prejudices against all Buddhas and Lamas, and place a high value on pure thoughts. Never leave such a state even for a second; devote yourself. Seek ablution from above and chant repeatedly, and unite your heart and your will. Do not get confused by your doubts, and hold to right wisdom only. This is the essence of my advice, so follow it.

I will send you blessings from the pure land and guide the future generations. Stop unnecessary grieving and offer prayers. I will be happy if you follow the divine Dharma. I will keep looking after you until you attain the Buddhahood. I pray that happiness and prosperity may be with you.

As he spoke thus, the child turned into a shaft of light with the colours of a rainbow and dissolved into the landscape. During this time the people were full of anguish like fish thrown onto a sandy beach, crying out prayers into empty space. Pema Tang was re-named Bub Tang (the land of the pitfall) after the event when the Lama's horse came out of the pitfall and stood there. They filled the hole with jewels and grain, and placed the rock with the marking of the body face down. A stupa was built on top of the watch post in the chief's mansion, and the Lama's cremated remains and ashes were placed inside. A three-day memorial service is conducted there every year.

The rock with clear markings on it that hit the Lama's right elbow, was found where the horse fell, and was considered to be a sign of Palden Sangmo's repentance. It was carried out and laid on the round platform built in front of the mansion. Palden Sangmo prayed there almost everyday, and she attained enlightenment during her lifetime.

This is the story of Gere Lama's murder as told by the Dakini, and it makes up the first half of the text. In the second half, Gere Lama himself tells his own life to Tulshuk Lingpa.

A monologue of Tulshuk Lingpa:

I was troubled by what I had seen in my dreams and in reality. I was wondering whether there was a detailed biography of Gere Lama, and was also asked to write a biography of the Lama by my attendants, sons and disciples. Just at this time, a rainbow light appeared in the sky in front of me at dawn the night after I arrived at the monastery in Patanam village, and Syunnu Senge (Gere Lama), a saint of about sixteen years of age, emerged from it.

A little flush came into his white skin and a tuft of his hair was braided. Wearing meditation codes and old white cotton clothes, carrying a *vajra*-pounder in his right hand

and holding a skull cup full of sweet nectar in his left hand, he spoke at ease as follows:

Oh great being, I will tell you the simple story of my life, the life of Syunnu Senge, so that you may tell others about it.

Gere Lama told Tulshuk Lingpa about his childhood, training and travels, and various episodes during his training.

I had finished learning to read and write and was already skilled at it when I was aged six, so I went to study with the great Guatsangpa and asked for the preliminary practices of the basic training and the four-part Tantra initiation. I stayed in Dilburi for five years.

After that, encouraged by my teacher, I spent one year going on pilgrimages to holy places in India. Then I established my sitting place on top of the mountain called Kanra, and for three years I held the victory flag of Buddhism there. I met the powerful saint Kanka Ripa there and completed the teachings of the exoteric and esoteric Tantra.

Additionally, I stayed in Asha and Sanling and spent one year at each of these localities, and gained a few good disciples. Following a hint from a Dakini, I went to Tibet and visited all the four regions in the U-Tsang (Central Tibet), in particular Gonla, Sakya, Kang Tise, Samye Chimpu, Lodak Karchu, Oruka, Dakpo, and Tsanran. I held the victory flag of Buddhism, followed the path of freedom, and spent a very happy seven years there.

After that I went to the Kathmandu Valley twice for missionary work, spending half a year there each time. I also stayed in Pange and Kashimir for more than a year. During these years, I accomplished much for Buddhism and sentient beings. I also practised mudra with the goddess of beauty and wisdom, the snake god and human women, and have become a person of insight beyond life.

An episode during his journey took place as follows:

When I was 35 years old, while practising in the Gere Mountain, many spirits came to invite me from a Beyul called the 'Land of No-Death'. At the Beyul, I turned the Wheel of Dharma for the spirits for three months.

There was immeasurable wealth and many treasures there. I brought back some seeds of barley and wheat from there and shared them with five households in the Tashigang, and in five years their harvest increased three-fold. At that time they used to call me 'Flying Lama'.

After telling about his life and his reincarnation during five generations, Gere Lama listed the names of the re-incarnations in the Mayul region who were his disciples or benefactors:

My prayers are efficacious and the vows of my followers are solid. People who have been associated for a long time now gather together here.

The one previously known as Tashi Palden is now called Katang. My senior disciple during my time in Asha was Dorje Sangpo. Now he is called Jangchub. Yeshe Sangpo at that time is now Purna Kirti. My brother Tshering Pal is now Pema Dechen. The chief Sonam Tobden is currently Tshering Namgyal. The sister of Tshering Pal, the chieftain of those days, is now called Lam. Gere Lama's favorite horse, the old black one, is now named Kanu. [Some passages omitted] Palden Sangmo of that time is now the woman named Chuki who lives near Bub Tang. All the others who saw or heard about the imprint of my body left on the rock or the story of my life, and believe it, are my disciples or faithful benefactors during my past life.

Most of the residents of this land, both men and women, were either my disciples or my benefactors. Even now I give them my compassion.

As noted earlier, the Mayul Valley has a significant number of Tulshuk Lingpa followers. The ones who believe the story of Gere Lama's *shabje* must of course be the followers of Tulshuk Lingpa. Therefore, Tulshuk Lingpa in this story comes to personify the existence of Gere Lama, and the link between Tulshuk Lingpa and his followers becomes intrinsically sanctified through the medium of Gere Lama. Even now his disciples who live in Lahul consider Tulshuk Lingpa to be a reincarnation of Gere Lama, and the people whose names were listed in the story were actual supporters of Tulshuk Lingpa who live around the Mayul Valley.

Gere Lama gave an ominous prophecy to Tulshuk Lingpa, which he introduced by telling him that the people would be able to drive away calamities by taking refuge in Buddhism for the next eight years.

On 10 June, build a stupa to appease Ulgyan Norla at the upper side of the valley. Build this stupa to exorcise evil spirits. Pierce the vital point that calms spirits. Use the powerful weapons of Dorje Phurpa to avoid the three troubles of illness, hunger and dispute. Build a stupa in the middle of the land without indulging in any gossip. Monks and lay persons, men and women, all should chant the mantra 'Mani Pagma Tan Vajra Guru'. Doing so will bring a luck to this land for the next eight years. Without your effort to avoid bad times, calamities will be worse from the Year of the Horse to the Year of the Sheep.

Not one person but many will die of illness. Evil that brings troubles will proliferate on the land and also dwell in people's hearts. People will not respect Buddhism; they will rather surrender themselves to sin. Their minds will be misled, and bad thoughts will dominate. Everyone will begin to believe the teachings of other religions. The teachings of the King will slowly decline.

Mountains will crumble, water will turn muddy, and years of agricultural failure will follow. The villagers will become slaves and the village will become empty. Even with the compassionate Three Jewels, it is difficult to compensate for bad deeds with blessings in bad times. No matter how much you try all kinds of means to counter them, it is difficult to rescue souls without faith and with deep doubt, so accept this and give up your suspicion. If you wish for happiness, give up duplicity and a distrusting heart. Give up doubt and initiate some plans for countering the bad situation. If you do this, you can unconditionally achieve peace for eight years.

However, he subsequently prophesied that calamities would be unavoidable.

From then on, the land will be covered by non-believers, and people's luck will be exhausted. In the Year of the Tiger, the world will sink in a sea of blood. No one will take refuge in the Three Jewels, and devils will be the leaders. Therefore, thoughtful people, seek the pure dharma and follow the words of truth in your heart. Give up prejudice against the Lama's words and actions. Pray to abandon doubt. Accumulate merit with prayers and donations. Always cherish your dislike of the impermanent world and be compassionate. Follow the ten good precepts, and be strict about your repentance and precepts. To gain happiness and merit in the present and future lives you should stay with the noble Lama, listen to his pure and true words of wisdom. The fortunate ones should do so without any reservations. Samaya.

Eight years from the Wood Horse Year (1954) when this prediction was the Year of the Tiger (1962). In this year Tulshuk Lingpa left Lahul in search of the Beyul and stayed in Sikkim and Darjeeling. As the prophesy of Gere Lama predicted that 'the world will sink into an ocean of blood', China and India engaged in a war over their borders and India suffered a terrible defeat.

In the last part of the text, Tulshuk Lingpa asked Gere Lama about Guru Yoga (the method of visualizing Lama during meditation). The biography ends with Gere Lama's replies to his questions.

The text seemed to be based on traditional accounts circulated around the Mayul Valley. However, it is cleverly constructed in that it first sets up Tulshuk Lingpa as the spokesperson for the episode of Gere Lama, and then eliminates the difference between the two in the end.

The accounts show that ascetics of the Ningma School often take the role of intermediary because they receive a message from a supernatural being, such as Padmasambhava, and communicate this to humans. From this viewpoint, some authors are of the opinion that they are a form of shaman.[8]

It is impossible to confirm whether Tulshuk Lingpa actually received a prophecy from Gere Lama during his trance, or whether he wilfully fabricated the text. However, by identifying Tulshuk Lingpa with Gere Lama, the text became the tool for self-mystification or self-justification, and for validating the relationship between him and his followers. Furthermore, it can be interpreted as a strategic arrangement for his journey in search of Beyul. This identification ended with an ironic twist of fate, owing to the unexpected death of Tulshuk Lingpa under an avalanche instead of in a pitfall.

ABOUT *BEYUL*

What was the Beyul that Tulshuk Lingpa tried to find at the literal risk of his life? Unfortunately, there is hardly anything left of his writing about it except for a short prayer.

In general, documents regarding Beyuls, especially the various guidebooks that exist, have been appearing since the fourteenth century, some of which refer to Demojōn, the Beyul that Tulshuk Lingpa was searching for.

Here I take up the subject of the guidebooks discovered by three famous Tertons of the Ningma School, in order to examine some concrete cases of Beyul. The books I will cover here are *The General Gate Sign of Beyul* (sbas yul spyi'i them byang bsyugs so), hereafter *Gate Sign*, discovered by Rigzin Gudem (rig 'dzin rgod ldem) (1337-1409),[9] *A Useful Guidebook on Beyul Demojon, Marvellous Buried Treasure* (sbas yul 'bras mo ljongs kyi gnas yig phan yon dang bcas pa ngo mtshar gter mdsod shes bya ba bsugs so) hereafter *Buried Treasure* discovered by Sangye Lingpa (sangs rgyas gling pa) (1340-96),[10] and *Guidebook for Beyul Demojon and Khempapalung* (sbas yul 'bras mo gshongs dang mkhan pa lung gi gnas yig bsyugs so) hereafter *Guidebook* discovered by Pema Lingpa (pad ma gling pa) (1450-?).[11]

All of these re-discovered books called *Guidebook to Beyul (Lamyig)* introduce King Tison Detsen (khri srong lde btsan) and princess Pema Se (pad ma gsal) in the era of the Tufan Kingdom who asks Padmasambhava questions about Beyul, and Padmasambhava answers them.

They initially mention the right time for the people to leave for Beyul.

In the words of Padmasambahava:

Oh Powerful King, listen now. First of all, follow Buddhism and do not be confused by trivial indications. Especially, when you have to leave for Beyul, the following signs will become apparent.

Most objects of worship in the temples built by three kings (Sontsen Gampo, Tison Detsen, and Titsuku Detsen, who heartily patronized Buddhism) will be destroyed. The temples of Tadul (mtha' 'dul) and Yandul (yang 'dul) will decline.[12] There will be no benefactors, but two generations from now an incarnated king will begin building a temple in the land of Do. During the 360-year period after the construction of that temple, it will be destroyed and turned into ruins.

These are external signs that are connected to the land, which indicate the time to leave for a Beyul.

As for the internal signs, the power of the Tibetan king will be weakened and the social order will be destroyed. Tibet's disorder will continue for 129 years.

It will be subjugated by the Black Mudur Hor (mu dur nag po hor). The subjugation will last for 125 years and then the domination of the Hor will also collapse. At that time the people of Tibet will have to go to a Beyul. (*Gate Sign*: 464-6).

The *Guidebook* has this to say on the matter:

People will suddenly die of stomach pain. The king will lack authority and his subjects will not pay attention to him. People will not have dignity and will become just like dogs. The sun will not shine on the land and will become like a desert. People will not be taken into consideration and become just like ghosts. There will be no leisure and life will be like a dark night. There will be no wealth in the household which will be felt like an empty shelter. People will be subjected to unprecedented and evil slave labor. When such a time comes, then escape to a Beyul. (*Guidebook*: 496-7)

The *Gate Sign* reads:

The time when people should leave for a Beyul is the time of disgrace when society is in chaos and people's faith and morals have declined. In such a time, people will become envious of one another and fight, and monks will carry swords inside their robes. Even women will be killed with knives, and anyone who still lives will have to hide in a burrow. (*Gate Sign*: 470)

The texts say that when the internal situation in Tibet will be in such disorder there will be invaders from foreign lands. These forces, called Tama (mtha' dmag), will be Hor, Chinese (rgya mi) and Muslims (du ru ka). In particular, there are many descriptions concerning the threat of Hor (the term Hor applies to different people depending on the period: in this case seems to refer to the Mongols):

The rule of Ghingis Khan will begin. Strong men will be killed and walls of flesh will be built. Women will become slaves and men will be slaughtered. How miserable the Tibetan people will be. (*Guidebook*: 499)

One of the above-mentioned passages in the *Guidebook* states that when the rule of Hor is imposed, it will be time to leave for Beyul. This was the time when Rigzin Gudem, Sangye Lingpa, and later Pema Lingpa, who discovered the guidebooks to Beyul, lived. Beyuls were the places prepared to escape internal turmoil and external invaders.

Beyuls are located in several places within and around Tibet.

There are some hidden countries within the southern region from Khunglung Dakar (khungs lung brag dkar) of Guge (gu ge) to Lonthan Donma (klong thang sgron ma) of the Do Khams (mdo khams) area. The three largest countries are Tsari (rtsa ri) in the east, Demojon ('bras mo gshongs) in the south and Demoku ('bras mo khugs) in the north. Thirteen mid-sized countries are located in the southern area between Tsawerong of Gyamo (rgya mo tsha ba'i rong) and Sa Lum of Tsan (gtsang sra rum). (*Gate Sign*: 476)

The geographical distribution of the Beyuls is supposed to be mainly concentrated in the Himalayan mountains in southern Tibet, along the current borders with India, Sikkim, Nepal and Bhutan.

According to the *Gate Sign* discovered by Rigzin Gudem, the Beyul called Tsari is supposed to be located at the western side of the bend of the Yarlung Tsangpo River. Demojon, which Tulshuk Lingpa tried to discover, is very famous and known as 'the King of Beyuls'. Sikkim is also called Demojon or Dejon, and it is said that an undiscovered Beyul is still hidden somewhere near Kanchenjunga. Demojon is also called the 'Country Between' because it lies between Tibet and Mon (Bhutan). (*Buried Treasure*: 16)

Also, a Beyul called Yolmogang (yol mo gangs) is believed to be situated in the area of Dingri near the Nepalese border in Tibet and another one, Kenpalung (mkhan pa lung), to the south of Mt. Everest.[13]

Although not mentioned in the *Gate Sign*, Beyul Pemako is in the east where the bend of the Yarlung Tsangpo River is located, and the other Beyul, Kimo Lung (skyid mo lung) is located in present-day Nepal, between Ganesh Himal and Manaslu.

There is no explanation why most Beyuls are set in southern locations, away from the basin of the Yarlung Tsangpo that forms the geographical centre of Tibet. However, since Beyuls are places of refuge from the invasions of northern tribes, it may be natural for them to be located in the south. One southern Beyul, the Demojon that Tulshuk Lingpa sought, was an especially important one.

Build eight temples at the border of the continuous Kanchenjunga (khangs chen mdsod lnga) in Taktseri, in the south of Tibet. Set up sangha. Prepare the road for Demojon. Build a temple in the center of this holy land.

From the east the outside invaders will sweep U Tsang three times. However, the fire of war will not reach the remote Loka [Southern Tibet] region. At this time, the people who remember me (Padmasambhava) will set out on the search for Beyuls, fortified by the power of their faith. Later, all the residents of U-Tsang will escape from the Hor army and immediately leave Tibet for Demojon to be free from the hand of evil. (*Gate Sign*: 482-3)

The *Buried Treasure* discovered by Sangye Lingpa is a guidebook to Beyul Demojon, and it emphasizes the material wealth and ease that will be gained in Demojon.

In the lower land of the 'Between Country', Demojon, there are three valleys where wheat grows by itself. In the middle land, there are three valleys where barley grows by itself and further, there are seventy-five valleys where anything planted will grow. (*Buried Treasure*: 25)

A diet of meat creates a special dilemma for the Tibetan people who must comply with the Buddhist rule that forbids the killing of sentient beings, but this problem is solved in Demojon.

In the south of Demojon, there is a valley called San San Lung. The valley has a mouth, and the shape of the headwater spreads out like the fingers of an opened hand. Thirty kinds of animals live in this place. Most of the animals in Demojon will come and die there, so there is an endless supply of carcasses. People who want meat can get it there.

When you eat meat, give offerings to the Tsen, the gods dwelling in the valley. This is known as the 'Buried Treasure' of meat. However, persecuting or harming animals which live in the valley is not allowed. As long as you do not persecute or harm animals, you will be able to have meat continuously. (*Buried Treasure*: 72-3)

The geographical formation of Demojon and its hidden treasure are detailed in *Buried Treasure*:

The headwaters of the 'Between Country', Demojon, are located in the direction of the Five Treasure Taktse. From there a glacier with seven branching valleys flows down. Deer, gowa (unknown), rock sheep, wild mice, goats, snow chicken, and zegpa (a kind of wild bird) frolic in the headwater area. The mouth of the valley is located in the direction of Wan Tsan. Tigers, puma, bears, dee (a kind of bear?), and maja (a kind of bird . . . peacock?) are found there.

Rinchenjong in the mid-stream area is similar to a gold platter filled with oil. There are 125 small valleys, and the mouths of every valley meet in one location. It takes four days on horseback to go from the source of the valley to the mouth. (*Buried Treasure*: 19)

There is a chunk of salt ore with a height and width of 20 mats called 'White Pure Salt Rock' in the northeast of Rinchenjong, within the snow mountain of Five Treasure Taktse, on the eastern wing. . . . The first snow mountain is the treasure house of salt. The second snow mountain is the treasure house of gold and turquoise. The third snow mountain is the treasure house to increasing Buddhist teaching and wealth. The fourth snow mountain is the treasure house of weapons. The fifth snow mountain is the treasure house of grains and medicines. (*Buried Treasure*: 64-5)

Also, in the north of Demojon is the valley where cooking utensils are buried, in the east is the valley where cotton and wool grow, in the south is the valley where you can get meat, and in the west is a cave where Buddhist ceremonial tools such as drums, flutes, conch shells, bells and chimes are stored. (*Buried Treasure*: 71-6)

Material wealth emphasizes Beyul's utopian characteristics. However, the vision of social life in Demojon described in the *Buried Treasure* is rather conservative.

Beyul, Rinchen Demojon has many residents from the four horns of U-Tsang. Nomads with their tents live in the high land, meditation places and temples are located in the middle land, and farmers live and build their villages in the low land. There is no one without possessions, and most of the people who live there have their own property.

The king must be someone born in the Year of the Boar. People born in the Year of the Tiger and the Year of the Monkey are eligible to be monks, those born in the Year of the Horse and the Year of the Snake are eligible to be esoteric ascetics, and those born in the Years of the Chicken, Bull and Snake are eligible to be queens. Those born in the Years of the

Dog, Dragon and Sheep are eligible to be cabinet members.

Everyone who gathers there must obey the orders of one king and live according to the precepts and must take care because mistakes will cause difficulties.

When you first arrive there, live on what grows there naturally. During that time, make preparations to build houses and temples and planting crops, so that you will be able to live on the harvest. In that land the harvest of the grain is extremely plentiful. If you plant one de of seeds, you will have a harvest of 20 ke. (*Buried Treasure*: 48-9)

It is clear from this text that a Beyul is not a kind of utopian movement where a reverse image of the existing social system is offered as a protest against it. In other words, there is not much of a revolutionary orientation in the sense of 'seeking a fundamental transformation of the social system or the social organization' in the motivation of the search for a Beyul.[14]

Both on the journey to Beyul, and once living there, it is also impossible to avoid interacting with various local gods. In *Buried Treasure*, there are many descriptions about the various manifestations of gods as well as advice about how to deal with them.

If you have the problem of a tiger in the 'Between Country' Demojon, offer a white yak which is a transformation of the mountain god Zunga Taktsema. If you cannot come up with a white yak, then make a yak effigy made of butter, and offer it using a stick so that all his sense organs are sticking out. Write the spell 'Om vi ta vi te phurna bajra hum pat' on a white silk cloth, recite it 108 times to welcome the god, then place it on his right shoulder and you will escape the problem of the tiger.

When you encounter the problem of a poisonous snake, this is due to the transformation caused by the anger of the snake god called Yum Rumo Sermikmo. . . . (*Buried Treasure*: 77-8)

The Ningma School to which the Tertons belong to professes itself to be an esoteric sect of Buddhism brought from India in the Tufan era by Padmasambhava, Vimalamitra and Vailochana. However, the school also survived by suiting to a popular taste for shamanistic magic and by integrating various elements of folk religions.

Images of Beyul are also based on the native spiritual culture of Tibet that was present before the arrival of Buddhism and has co-existed along with Buddhist culture, while sometimes being antagonistic, yet partly blending together.

The Beyul also functions as a holy place that purifies the people who visit it.

In Demojon, the virtues one should look for and the happiness of sentient beings arise spontaneously. Experiences and insights arise within one's power. People who arrive there early will attain the supreme achievement of enlightenment. People who arrive there during the middle time will attain common achievements. Even those who arrive late will be freed from the savage state. (*Buried Treasure*: 91)

That land is the palace for spiritual teachers, meditational deities, sky-goers, heroes and heroines. Its valleys, snowy mountains, lakes, caves and tree trunks are palaces of the gods. It is the real Buddha field, and not only for people who go and live there. Even people who hear about Demojon can accumulate immeasurable merits. People who are willing to go there possess good karma and fortune. People who actually go there are reincarnated Bodhisattvas on the Bodhisattva grounds. If you make a pilgrimage to Demojon, all of your non-virtues and obscurations accumulated since a long time will be purified.

If you live there, at best, you will go to the Buddha field without abandoning the illusory body made of the four elements. At the middle level, you will be able to realize the meaning of emptiness of the mind and thus attain enlightenment. Even in the worst case, you will be able to attain enlightenment at the first Bardo. By just seeing the land, the door to the three bad worlds will be closed. (*Buried Treasure*: 93-4)

If you practice in the land (Khenpajong), you will be able to live until the age of one hundred years and to achieve the state of accomplished tantric practitioner in the next rebirth. I (Padmasambhava) will bestow initiation upon anyone who meditates, regardless of whether that person is a man or a woman. He or she will be shown the Dharma and the scriptural teachings.

Anyone who meditates on the nature of fundamental Clear Light will enjoy the blessing of unsurpassable goodness. Just by living on the land, the obstacles to liberation formed by disturbing attitudes and emotions will be spontaneously purified. Love and compassion will arise naturally for every resident who lives there. His knowledge will increase and will shine.

Practising for one year in this land is much better than practising for a thousand years in other localities. Practising for one month in this land is better than practising for one year in other localities. Practising for three days here is better than practising for one month in other localities. (*Guidebook*: 520)

The following prayer composed by Tulshuk Lingpa indicates that his journey to Beyul was actually nothing less than a kind of pilgrimage to the Holy Land.

Prayer to reach Beyul: I request my spiritual teachers, the Three Jewels and the Three Roots (Lama, Protector God, Dakini), especially to the Hero of Ulgyan (Padmasambhava), the sky-goers (Dakini), the Dharma protectors, and the gods of wealth, the protectors who should be bound to an oath and the lords of treasure.

Please bless us to accomplish what we wish. May we surely and without any obstacle arrive at these Holy Lands, including the major eight Beyuls such as Pemako, Lhomon, Demojon, Chirita that are equal to the Pure Land of Great Bliss, as we all are sincerely faithful. May our wishes be accomplished without any obstacles. May we achieve the transformation into the Rainbow Body in this lifetime by practising the unsurpassable Vajra Vehicle (Tantrayana).

MEANING OF THE SEARCH FOR BEYUL

Although Tulshuk Lingpa's quest ended in catastrophe, why were so many people of Lahul attracted to the vision that Tulshuk Lingpa presented? To answer this question, we need to consider the characteristics of Lahuli society and the social and historical context in which the people of Lahul were placed during that time. I will outline some of these issues.

First, let us consider the structural aspects of Lahuli society.

As I have noted earlier, the behavioural characteristics of Lahuli people can be understood in terms of the dynamics between the concentration-oriented household, *kyum*, and the diffusion-oriented family, *jinmad*. Although they have attached great importance to gathering family wealth together and concentrating their capital for the household, they also have engaged in various outside economic activities. Lahuli Society has taken advantage of profitable investment opportunities beyond its regional boundaries, by assigning male members of the family to these activities.

This entrepreneurial spirit of the Lahuli society has contributed greatly to the improvement of their economic status as it exists today.

The quest for Beyul was essentially a religious movement led by a personality called Tulshuk Lingpa, but at least for those who participated in it, it was also a practical immigration movement. It was reported that many people who joined in the search for Beyul disposed of their properties upon their departure. It was not only an act of determination but also a practical move, since they would need to build a new village when they reached the new land. From that perspective, one can especially see similarities with the spirits of the Lahuli people who ventured out of Lahul after 1970 in search of profitable investment opportunities.

On the other hand, the early 1960s when Tulshuk Lingpa's Beyul search was going on also happened to be a time of social upheaval in the areas surrounding Lahul. For instance, when the Republic of India was formed in 1950 and more than a hundred years of British colonial rule came to an end, the power of the old lords who were the actual rulers in Lahul under British control was stripped away.

In 1959, the political power of the Dalai Lama of Tibet, who was semi-independent until then, was completely destroyed during the Lhasa uprising. Subsequently, the Dalai Lama was forced to flee to India.

Lahul has never been under the power of the Dalai Lama. However, for these people who speak a dialect of the Tibetan language as their mother tongue, and embrace Tibetan Buddhism, and depend on Tibetan medicine, or the Tibetan calendar, the collapse of Tibet must have caused a strong sense of crisis. Also, from an economic perspective, the closing of the Tibetan border with India meant the loss of a long-time trading partner.

Also, in 1962 the India-China border dispute broke out and both armies went into battle over the McMahon Line in eastern India, and the territory of Aksaychin near Lahul on the western side. As noted previously, 1962 was the year that Tulshuk Lingpa predicted the world would sink into a sea of blood.

Tulshuk Lingpa's search for Beyul can be thought of as a general example of a utopian movement that emerges at a turning point in a societies history.

However, when comparing the search for Beyul with typical utopian movements such as the Millennium Kingdom Movement in Melanesia that emerged under colonial control, there seems to be an essential difference.

According to Peter Worsley,

> The millenarian cult may thus be seen not as an irrational flight from reality or a regression from the present into the past but as a quite logical interpretation and criticism of a European-controlled order that is full of contradictions which seem inexplicable in rational terms to the natives.[15]

In contrast, during the activities that led to the search for Beyul by Tulshuk Lingpa, I do not see anyone taking a truly prophetic role that would generate new values during the transitional period in the society to which Turner refers.[16] Just as Aries called the famous Terton Pama Lingpa a 'Buddhist shaman', the role of a Terton is not that of a prophet who creates a new value himself, but of a shaman who receives messages of great saints of the past through spiritual contact, and then communicates them to the people.[17]

The Beyul that Tulshuk Lingpa sought is, more than anything else, the land where people could escape the aggression of invaders and social chaos. Also by reaching that land the people could achieve higher religious merits. In that sense, the search for Beyul was none other than a kind of pilgrimage to holy lands.

Many guidebooks on Beyul, including the one discovered by Rigzing Gudem, note various signs that indicate the timing of departure for Beyul. According to them, the time to leave for Beyul is indicated by social disorder, the decline of Buddhism, increasingly corrupt morals and the beginning of aggression by foreign invaders. For Tulshuk Lingpa and his followers, the social upheaval of Indian society at the time, the Chinese invasion of Tibet and its hasty advance to the Indian border all must have been interpreted as the exact signs for the time of departure for Beyul.

The number of disciples who followed Tulshuk Limgpa from Lahul was equalled or exceeded by the number of people from Sikkim and Bhutan who joined him in the search for Beyul. This indicates not only that the Tibetan cultural frontier area which spreads throughout the southern face of the Himalayas shares the same religious foundation as Lahul, but also how large an impact the collapse of Tibet and the following confusion had on the region.

Looking at the consequences of pilgrimage, their search for Beyul may have ended as a harrowing failure. However, that event conceals the resilience of the Lahuli society that will advance into the outside world upon the first opportunity, just as the bent bamboo will snap. It also gives an account of their potential power, which includes their sincere aspiration to attain spiritual heights.

NOTES

1. Tselam is located at the upper part of a valley that stretches toward the south-west from the peak of Kanchenjunga.
2. The names of the fifty Tertons are listed in (Tucci, 1980, pp. 258-9).
3. Yamaguchi, 1988, p. 65.
4. A large stupa and a temple were built by disciples in Telin village where Tulshuk Lingpa once lived. A cave where he practised still remains in Pangan in Kullu, and is now a monastery for the Ningma School.

5. This book was edited and published by Khasdub Gyatsho of Manali in 1997 from the texts used by Tulshuk Lingpa. It consists of 56 chapters with 302 pages of texts. It includes texts written by Tulshuk Lingpa and Dorje Dechen Lingpa amongst them.
6. There is an English translation of this text by Mullin (Mullin, 1986).
7. The personal history of Kumara Senha or Gere Lama, and the fact of whether or not he actually existed, is unknown.
8. Aris has discussed the difference between the orthodox Siberian shaman who dissociates his soul and the Terton who becomes possessed (Aris, 1988, p. 60). However, a Terton's contact with a supernatural being is made in his dreams, and this is a little different from a possessed shaman whose body is taken over by a god or various spiritual beings (Sasaki, 1992, p. 154).
9. Rigzing Gudem is known for discovering Jan Ter or the 'Northern Buried Scripture'. His full name was Rigzing Chenpo Ngudup Gyaltsen but he is called Rigzing Gu Ki Demu Tu Chen or Rigzing Gudem. His name originates from three eagle feathers that grew on his head when he was eleven years old, and five eagle feathers that grew on his head when he was twenty-three years old (Gu is Eagle, Demu Tu means feather ornaments). In 1336 he discovered a wooden box with five parts in a cave called San San Ra Dah. Many important religious texts were stored in that box and these texts are called the *Five Treasures.* He was also known for finding a key to open the seven most important Beyul, and another key for discovering a list of buried scriptures (Dargyay, 1977, pp. 129-31). *Gate Sign* is one of these texts that was found in San San Ra Dah, according to its postscript. It contains a wealth of information about Beyul in Tibet and their surrounding areas, including their locations, the time for departure, and the means for getting there. This is probably the most well-known text about Beyul. The text I used here consists of 17 pages and is a copy of the Ume calligraphy style.

10. Sangye Lingpa was born in the Nyang region of Konpo in 1340 and was later named Rigzin. After his father died during his childhood, he suffered neglect by his mother's new husband. He became a monk at a monastery near Tsari and was called Sangye Sampo. He had a vision of Avalokitesvara and Padmasambhava in Lhasa. One night he received three pieces of paper that indicated the location of a buried scripture from a guardian god. In 1364 he also discovered an important scripture, with the help of Padmasambhava and a Dakini. After that his search continued, and he discovered many more scriptures and sacred objects. When he was in search of buried scriptures, flowers often fell like rain showers, a dome-like rainbow appeared, music could be heard and Dakinis appeared (Dargyay, 1977, pp. 132-35). The text I used here consists of 68 pages of wood block prints in the Uchen calligraphy style. However, *Buried Treasure* makes up only 53 out of these 68 pages; other excerpts from the texts of Rigzing Gudem and Pema Lingpa are included. According to the postscript, a person named La Tsun Gyurme had compiled it on request from the people of Sikkim.
11. Pema Lingpa is the fourth of the five 'Terton Kings' and is considered to be a reincarnation of Pema Se, a daughter of King Tison Detsen. He was born in 1450 in Bumtang in Mon (present-day Bhutan). He was not only highly intellectual but also talented in many kinds of crafts, including blacksmith work. When he was 27 years old, he obtained a list of 108 great buried scriptures. His first discovery was performed in the 'Blazing Lake of Fire'. He was submerged into water in front of many people holding a butter lamp in his hand, and emerged holding a box containing scriptures. It was said that his butter lamp was not affected. He continued his search and discovered many more scriptures and treasures. According to legend, he left a prophesy that he would be reborn as a Buddha in a Beyul called Pema Ko, and that his disciples would also be reborn and liberated in the same land (Dargyay, 1977, pp. 147-50). For more details on life

of Pama Lingpa, please refer to (Aris, 1988). The first half of the *Guidebook* describes Beyul Demojon, and the later half describes Kenpajon. However, the part on Demojon was clearly borrowed from *Buried Treasure* by Sangye Lingpa. The text I used here consists of 49 pages in the Uchen calligraphy style. The following books contain printed copies of these impressions; Ngawang Topgyal (ed.), *Collected GTER-MA Rediscoveries of Padma-Glin-pa*; a reproduction of a rare manusucript from the Manang collection, vol. 3.

12. Eight temples built by King Sontsen Gampo for appeasing Tibetan gods (Kunga Dorje, 1964, p. 92).
13. Reinhard, 1978.
14. Hobsbaum, 1989, p. 42.
15. Worsley, 1968, p. 242.
16. Turner, 1976.
17. Aris, 1988, p. 59.

CHAPTER 9

Conclusion

Above the village of Kardang there is a small monastery called Kardang Gonpa that belongs to the Kagyu School of Tibetan Buddhism. Besides the main temple, the adjunct kitchen and individual living quarters for monks and nuns stand side by side in the back. In general it is very rare to see monks and nuns living in the same monastery, but in the case of Kardang Gonpa, the ratio of ordained men to women is half and half, most of whom come from Kardang and the surrounding villages.

In antiquity, a temple once stood where the present Gonpa is located, but it is now in ruins and has been abandoned for many years. In 1912 a monk from Kardang village named Norbu (1885-1947) built the new temple at the site.

He travelled to the faraway land of the Kham together with others such as the Yoga practitioner Kunga (1884?-1967), and received teaching from Thukutan Syakyashiri (rtogs ldan sha'kya shri) (1853-1919), who belonged to the Kagyu School and was knowledgeable about the teachings of the Ningma School. The circumstances of Norbu becoming a disciple of Thukutan Syakyashiri are not clear. However, according to legend, one day Thukutan Syakyashiri received a mysterious revelation that he had a follower in Lahul, so he sent his senior disciple there. According to Stuchbury, 18 people from Lahul travelled to Kham four times during the ten years preceding the death of Syakyashiri in 1919.[1] In fact, a biography of Syakyashiri refers to, among his disciples, several names of Lahul origin, together with Kunga and Norbu.

At the time, Kham was known as the centre of the Rime (ris med) religious movement and Thukutan Syakyashiri was one of its central figures.

Rime was a non-sectarian religious movement that emerged around Derge in eastern Tibet during the nineteenth century. People who participated in the Rime movement relied mainly on the teaching traditions of Dzogchen of the Ningma School, and Chakchen of the Kagyu School, yet in principle they acted without prejudice towards other sects. The great scholars of Rime such as Kontul (kong sprul) (1811-99), Kentse Wangpo (mkhyen brtse dbang po) (1820-92) and Mipąm Gyamtso (mi pham rgya mtsho) (1846-1912) wrote extensive works, and contributed greatly to projects devoted to publishing ancient Buddhist scriptures.[2]

Syakyashiri received teachings from the foremost scholars of the Rime movement including Kentse Wongpo and Mipam Gyamtso, who was knowledgeable about the teachings of Dzogchen and Chakchen. One time he even served as the abbot of the famous Kato Gonpa of the Ningma School.

Incidentally, Tulshuk Lingpa's master Ngawang Pelsan (also known as Pema Lerde Tse) was a friend of Kato Situ Cyuki Gyamtso (ka' thog si tu chos kyi rgya mtsho) (1880-1925), who was a disciple of Syakyashiri. Kato Situ Cyuki Gyamtso wrote a biography (namthar) of Syakyashiri after his death, and is also known for a travel account he composed during his pilgrimage from Kham to central Tibet.

Norbu built five temples in India including Kardang Gonpa, and in his later years he lived in Zonkul Gonpa in Zanskar until his death.

After Norbu's passing away, his reincarnation was identified as the son of a disciple of Syakyashiri outside Lhasa. Messengers were sent from Kardang Gonpa several times inviting him to visit. However, the young reincarnation of Norbu did not leave Tibet. In the meantime, Tibet was invaded by China. Ultimately the reincarnation of Norbu chose the life of a layman, and he is still living in Tibet.

The fate of so many Tibetans underwent violent changes due to the Chinese occupation of Tibet. Norbu's teacher, Abo Rinpoche, the grandson of Syakyashiri, was one of thousands of Tibetans who escaped to exile in India following the 1959 Lhasa Uprising. Buddhists of Lahul and Kullu invited him to stay and supported him as a master.

Abo Rinpoche died in 1974. His son, Se Rinpoche (Ngawang Gele Namgyal) was recognized as the reincarnation of a high ranking monk. He married a young woman from Kardang and now lives in Manali. Monks and Nuns of Kardang Gompa honour Se Rinpoche as the descendant of Norbu's teacher Syakyashiri.

Some time in Norbu's later years, the Terton from Amdo, Tulshuk Lingpa, was a visitor to Lahul. The woman saint who encouraged him to go to India, Shunsep Jetsun Lochen, spent her twenties wandering in western Tibet, and Lahul.

Lochen was born to a Tibetan father and a Nepali mother in 1865 in Tso Pema, the holy Tibetan Buddhist pilgrimage site near Mandi in Himachal Pradesh.

According to Lochen's biography,[3] before she was born her mother prayed for a boy and made pilgrimages to the holy land of Avalokitesvara in Lahul carrying a rock on her back. Lochen's father came from a prestigious Cyongye family in central Tibet, but he was a severe alcoholic and abused Lochen and her mother whenever he was drunk.

With her terrible life as a child, Lochen became attracted to religious experiences at a tender age, and the mother and child used to make a living by singing religious songs, chanting the lore of saints, and wandered various regions of western Tibet including Lahul, Spiti, Zanskar, Ladakh, and Guge. In western Tibet, Lochen is the name given to people who make a living by singing religious songs.

It was not long before Lochen met her life-long master, the yoga ascetic Pema Gyamtso, and joined his religious community. Later Pema Gyamtso and his party made a pilgrimage to western Tibet and Nepal, before going to Lhasa.

After going through many mystical experiences, Lochen gradually became well-known in central Tibet. Nobles and wealthy merchants, and even a high Lama of a religious order, paid visits to Shunsep, her base located in the south-west of Lhasa, in order to receive her teachings. The monastery of Shunsep remained a nunnery after her passing away but was severely damaged during the Chinese occupation.

Most of Lochen's teachers, including Pema Gyamtso, came from Kham or Amdo, and she herself belonged to Rime lineage.

Lahul is nestled deep in the valleys of the Himalayan mountains, and like a Beyul, is a hidden land itself. It belongs to the vast Tibetan cultural area that used to extend to central Asia, that was a land frequented by various religious masters including Norbu, Tulshuk Lingpa, Lochen, pilgrims and merchants.

The power of the religious movement that emerged in eastern Tibet was transmitted to Lahul at the western edge of the Tibetan cultural sphere by these travellers, thereby awakening the people's religious passion. Indeed, religious activities in Lahul in the twentieth century, like

Norbu's founding of Kardang Gonpa and the Beyul exploration led by Tulshuk Lingpa, were inspired by and had their origins in the Rime movements of eastern Tibet.

However, the conditions that influence Lahul's socio-political and religious traditions have been changing dramatically over the last several decades. The once vast Tibetan cultural area that Lahul once and almost exclusively belonged to has been torn apart by the geopolitical strategic ambitions of modern states. In the meantime, with the dramatic transformation of Indian society since Independence, Lahul has become increasingly subject to its overpowering influence.

Even compared with my first visit to Lahul in the late 1980s, the scale of recent changes there is astonishing. For example, electronic appliances such as televisions are now found in every household, and modern equipment is used for traditional tasks such as making butter. Telephones were installed in the village several years ago, and in the town of Keylong across the river from Kardang, it is now even possible to use the internet.

Barley and buckwheat which were grown ten years ago are rarely planted now; in their place are cash crops such as potatoes and green peas. This change indicates how Lahuli society has abandoned its old traditions of self-sufficiency and become increasingly dependent on a market economy.

That is not all. The influence of Tibetan Buddhism re-established by Norbu and others is again showing signs of decline. For example, the number of new monks that enter Kardang Gonpa has been decreasing over the years. As a consequence of this, year 2000, Cham (a religious theatre with masked dancers) could not be staged as scheduled, because there was not the requisite number of monks required to perform.

In addition, children who are educated in the Indian school system speak English and Hindi, and have Hindu names along with their original Tibetan names. Now it is only monks and elders who used to trade across the Tibetan border who are able to understand a certain level of the Tibetan language.

It is impossible to avoid recognizing the overwhelming influence of modern Indian society in Lahul. Yet, as a whole, the people of Lahul have maintained the core values of the Tibetan social system and its sense of values up to the present day, and have successfully adapted to the modern changes.

A traditional society that has evolved over a long period of time is often equipped with a social system and set of values that are suitable, and in a sense natural, to its environment. One implication of the term 'natural' is that the system has a continuous economic cycle of production-distribution-consumption. Another is that it possesses various cultural mechanisms for regulating human relations, so that the relationships of people who live there will not fall apart. As has been argued throughout this book, the criteria and beliefs surrounding the household, family or gender issues, along with the economic systems, have in totality formed a self-sufficient system.

However, the circumstances in which modern Lahuli society finds itself; namely, the total penetration of the market economy and the rapid influx of Indian and Western values, are forcing the people of Lahul to restructure their traditional society.

This transition, from a traditional social system and set of values, to a modern society with all that it entails, raises a fundamental question. Specifically, which values will they abandon, and which values will they preserve during this process of restructuring their lives.

NOTES

1. Stutchbury, 1994, p. 168.
2. Yamaguchi, 1988, pp. 325-7; E. Gene Smith, 1969, 1970.
3. Lochen wrote a *namthar*, a kind of autobiography, during her later years. For Lochen's autobiography, please refer to Tanase, 2000. Also, Hanna Havnevik completed an English translation of the Lochen autobiography, except for religious songs (Havnevik, 1999).

Bibliography

ENGLISH WORKS

Aris, M., 1979, *Bhutan: The Early History of a Himalayan Kingdom*, Warminster: Aris and Phillips.

——1988, *Hidden Treasures and Secret Lives*, Shimla: Indian Institute of Advanced Study.

Aziz, B.N., 1978, *Tibetan Frontier Families*, New Delhi: Vikas.

Bengal Government Secretariat, 1972 (1894), *The Gazetteer of Sikkim*, New Delhi: Manjusri.

Blondeau, A.M., 1980, 'Analysis of the Biographies of Padma-sambhava According to Tibetan Tradition: Classification of Sources', in M. Aris and Aung San Suu Kyi, eds., *Tibetan Studies*, New Delhi: Vikas, pp. 45-52.

Brauen-Dolma, M., 1985, 'Millenarianism in Tibetan Religion', in B.N. Aziz and M. Kapstein, eds., *Tibetan Civilization*, New Delhi: Manohar, pp. 245-56.

Bray, J., 1998, 'The Contribution of the Moravian Mission to Tibetan Language and Literature', *Lungta*, 11, Dharamsala: Amnye Machen Institute, pp. 4-8.

Dargyay, E.M., 1979 (1977), *The Rise of Esoteric Buddhism in Tibet*, Delhi: Motilal Banarsidass.

Francke, A.H., 1907, *A History of Western Tibet*, London: S.W. Partridge.

——, 1962 (1914, 1926), *Antiquities of Indian Tibet* (2 vols.), New Delhi: S. Chand.

——, 1979 (1905), *History, Folklore & Culture of Tibet*, New Delhi: Ess Ess Publishers.

Fürer-Haimendorf, C. Von., 1964, *The Sherpa of Nepal*, Berkeley: University of California Press.

Gene Smith, E., 1969, 'A Preface to the Autobiographical Reminiscence of Ngag-dbang-dpal-bzang Late Abbot of Kah-thog Monastery', Gangtok.

——, 1970, 'An introduction to Kongtrul's Encyclopedia of Indo-Tibetan Culture', New Delhi: International Academy of Indian Culture.

Grierson, A.G., 1967 (1908), *Linguistic Survey of India*, vol. 3 (Part 1), Delhi: Motilal Banarsidass.

Havnevik, H., 1997, 'The Autobiography of Jetsun Lochen Rinpoche: A Preliminary Research Report', in Wrnest Steinkellner, ed., *Tibetyan Studies* (vol. 1), Wien: Verlag der Osterreichische Akademie der Wissenschaften, pp. 355-67.

——, 1988, 'On Pilgrimage for Forty Years in the Himalayas: The Female Lama Jetsun Lochen Rinpoche's (1865-1951) Quest for Sacred Sites', in Alex Mckay, ed., *Pilgrimage in Tibet*, Surrey: Curzon Press, pp. 85-107.

——, 1999, *The Life of Jetsun Lochen Rinpoche (1865-1951) As Told in Her Autobiography* (2 vols.), Oslo: Unipub, Akademika AS.

Hutchson, J. and J.P.H. Vogel, 1982 (1933), *History of the Punjab Hill States*, Shimla: Director of Languages and Culture, Himachal Pradesh.

Jiro, Kawakita, 1950, *Cyoso no kuni*, Tokyo: Kobunsya.

——, 1966. Chibettozoku no issaitahukon (1), *Minzokuga-kukenkyu*, 33(1), pp. 11-27.

Jiro, Tanase, 1989, 'The Influence of the Introduction of New Crops on Lahuli Society', in Sadao Sakamoto, ed., *A Preliminary Report of the Studies on Millet Cultivation and its Agro-pastoral Culture Complex in the Indian Subcontinent*, Kyoto University, pp. 133-42.

Khasdup Gyatso Shasin, ed., 1977, *Collected Revelations (gter chos) and Writings of brtul-zugs-glin-pa*, Delhi: Jayyed Press.

Kim Yeshi and Acharya Tashi Tsering, 1991, 'The Story of a Tibetan Yogini, Shungsep Jetsun', *CHÖ YANG*, Dharamsala: Council of Religion and Cultural Affairs of H.H. the Dalai Lama, pp. 130-43.

Levine, N.E., 1981, 'The Theory of Ru Kinship: Descent and Status in a Tibetan Society', in Fürer-Haimendorf, ed., *Asian Highland Societies*, New Delhi: Sterling Publisher.

——, 1988, *The Dynamics of Polyandry*, Chicago: The University of Chicago Press.

Magmain, N.D., 1975, *Himachal Pradesh District Gazetteers–Lahul & Spiti*, Greater Punjab Press.

Mullin, G.H., 1986, *Death and Dying*, Boston: Routledge and Kegan Paul.

Mumford, S.R., 1986, *Himalayan Dialogue*, Wisconsin: The University of Wisconsin Press.

Nakane, Chie, 1966, 'A Plural Society in Sikkim: A Study of the Interrelations of Lepchas', in Fürer-Haimendorf, ed., *Caste and Kin in Nepal, India and Ceylon*, London: Asia Publishing Press.

Parry, J.P., 1979, *Caste and Kinship in Kangra*, New Delhi: Vikas.

Peter, Prince of Greece and Denmark, 1963, *A Study of Polyandry*, The Hague: Mouton.

Prats, R., 1980, 'Some Preliminary Considerations Arising from a Biographical Study of the Early GTER-STON', in M. Aris and Aun San Suu Kyi, eds., *Tibetan Studies*, New Delhi: Vikas, pp. 256-60.

Reinhard, J., 1978, 'Khembalung: The Hidden Valley', *Kailash*, 6 (no. 1), Kathmandu: Ratna Pustak Bhandar, pp. 15-35.

Roerich, G.H., 1988 (1949), *The Blue Annals*, Delhi: Motilal Banarsidass.

Samuel, G., 1993, *Civilized Shamans*, Washington and London: Smithsonian Institute Press.

Sharma, D.D., 1989, *Studies in Tibeto-Himalayan Language 2. Tribal Language of Himachal Pradesh* (part 1), Delhi: Mittal Publications.

Stuchbury, E., 1994, 'The Making of Gonpa: Norbu Rinpoche from Kardang and Kunga Rinpoche from Lama Gonpa', in G. Samuel, H. Gregory, and E. Stuchbury, eds., *Tantra and Popular Religion in Tibet*, New Delhi: Aditya Prakashan, pp. 155-204.

Tobdan, 1984, *History & Religion of Lahul*, New Delhi: Books Today.

Tucci, G., 1980 (1949), *Tibetan Painted Scrolls*, Kyoto: Rinsen Syoin.

Worsley, Peter, 1968, *The Trumpet Shall Sound*, New York: Schocken Books.

Wylie, T.V., 1962, *The Geography of Tibet According to the 'Dzam-gLing rGyas-Bshad*, Roma: Is.M.E.O. (Ser. 25).

JAPANESE WORKS

Hakamaya, Noriaki, 1989, 'Chonanha to nyoraizousisou', in *Chibetto bukkyo*, Tokyo: Iwanamishoten, pp. 119-52.

Jiro, Tanase, 1991, 'Todomarouto surumonoto utsuriyuku mono: Indo, Himachal Pradesshu syu, Rahoru keikoku no chibbetokei syakai niokeru ie to kazoku', *Minzokugakukenkyu*, 52(2), pp. 159-77.

——, 1992a, 'Rahoru no tochigami(jida) ni tsuite', *Chibetto bunka kekyukaihou*, 16(2), pp. 19-23.

——, 1992b, 'Rahoru no chiisaki kamigami tachi', *Chibetto bunka kenkyuukaihou*, 16(4), pp. 16-19.

——, 1993a, 'Kanchenjunga ni kieta yutopia: chibetto bukkyo ninmaha no gyojya, teruton turusyuku rinpa no beyulu tansakukou', *Minzokugakukenkyu*, 57(4), pp. 444-55.

——, 1993b, 'Rahoru no chiisaki kamigami tachi (2)', *Chibetto bunka kenkyuukaihou*, 17(1), pp. 19-23.

——, 1993c, 'Rahul oyobi Zanskar chiiki no kazokukeitai ni tsuite', *Chibetto bunka kekyukaihou*, 17(3), pp. 18-22.

——, 1997, 'Chusei chibetto no ninmaha bunken ni mirareru beyulu no kannen ni tsuite', *Ningenbunka*, 2, pp. 258-72.

——, 2000, 'Chibetto no joseiseijya no monogatari: syunsep jetsun rochen rinpoche jiden', *Joseishigaku*, 10, pp. 28-39.

Kaneko, Eiichi, 1986, 'Padomasanbaba to samuie dera', in Yamaguchi, Zuiho (ed.), *Chibetto no bukkyo to syakai*, Tokyo: Syunjusya, pp. 111-42.

Kawaguchi, Ekai, 1988, *Chibetto ryokoki* (5 vols), Tokyo: Kodansya.

Moriyasu, Takao, 1987, 'Chuou ajiasi no naka no chibetto', in Yasuhiko Nagano, and Musashi Tachikawa, eds., *Chibetto no gengo to bunka*, Tokyo: Tojushya, pp. 44-68.

Nakazawa, Shinichi, 1981, *Niji no kaitei*, Tokyo: Hirakawashuppan.

Sasaki, Kokan, 1992, *Syamanizumu no sekai*, Tokyo: Kodansya.

Sato, Hisashi, 1986, *Cyusei chibetto kenkyu*, Kyoto: Dohosya.

Takayama, Ryuzo, 1990, *Usinawareta chibettojin no sekai.*, Tokyo: Niccyushuppan.

Tanaka, Kimiaki, 1994, *Chomikkyo jirin tantora*, Osaka: Tohoshuppan.

Yamaguchi, Zuiho, 1987, 1988, *Chibetto* (2 vols.), Tokyo: Tokyodaigakushuppan.

Index